Electing the President, 2008

Electing the President, 2008

The Insiders' View

EDITED BY
KATHLEEN HALL JAMIESON

PENN

University of Pennsylvania Press

Philadelphia

Published by
University of Pennsylvania Press
Philadelphia, Pennsylvania 19104-4112

Printed in the United States of America on acid-free paper
10   9   8   7   6   5   4   3   2   1

Library of Congress Cataloging-in-Publication Data

Electing the president, 2008 : the insiders' view / edited by Kathleen Hall Jamieson.
    p.   cm.
  ISBN 978-0-8122-2096-4 (alk. paper)
  Includes index.
    1. Presidents—United States—Election—2008.   2. Political campaigns—United States—Case studies.   I. Jamieson, Kathleen Hall
JK526   2004 .E442   2009
324.973/0931—dc22   2009017225

Contents

Introduction

Kathleen Hall Jamieson

The election of 2008 was historic, consequential, and the outcome clear. The Electoral College tally showed a decisive Obama win, 365 to 173 votes.[1] The popular vote spread was wide as well, 69,297,997 to 59,597,520. After years of hand wringing by good government advocates, 2008 produced the highest turnout in the United States in decades, up by more than a percent over 2004.

The winner would face a country barreling toward a trillion-dollar deficit, a financial crisis unlike any since the Great Depression, a stock market below 9000, two long-lived and expensive wars, the symbol of the terrorist attack on 9/11, Osama bin Laden still on the loose, and a scientific consensus that urgent action was needed to address what the Democrats called "a planet in peril."

As voters cast their ballots in the general election of 2008, the notion, as Democratic nominee Barack Obama phrased it, that the election represented "a defining moment in history" seemed apt. At the top of each major party ticket was an individual different in important ways from past nominees. On November 4, 2008, a country in which the majority of voters were white and whose past included slavery, lynching, and Jim Crow elected a Harvard educated former community organizer who telegraphed his racial identity by saying that his father came from Kenya and mother from Kansas. Among the states Obama carried was Virginia, a fact that highlighted the distance the country had traveled since Richmond served as capital of the Confederacy with Virginia native Robert E. Lee at the head of the army of the South. The Democratic standard bearer telegraphed the symbolic significance of that change when he noted that "When I raise my hand and take that oath of office, I think that the world will look at us differently. . . . And millions of kids across this country will look at themselves differently."[2]

Generational politics were at play as well in 2008. Where Senator John McCain represented the Vietnam generation of Baby Boomers, Barack Obama had not been born when the first U.S. advisers entered that far away country. As a candidate twenty-five years younger than his Republican rival, a person of color, highly educated and a liberal, Obama's identity coincided with that of his most ardent supporters.

By contrast, at the top of the Republican ticket was a Vietnam War hero who had been tortured while a prisoner of the North Vietnamese in the "Hanoi Hilton." An important player in Washington politics since the Reagan era, McCain was also the second oldest person ever to seek a first term on a major party ticket. Only 1996 Republican nominee Bob Dole at 73 was older than 72-year-old McCain.

The 2008 presidential election was unusual for other reasons as well. In every presidential year from 1952 through 2004, at least one party had featured a nominee tethered to the title president or vice president. And in the country's history, a nominating contest had never come down to either an African American or a woman finalist, much less both. The fact that the heads of the two parties came to the race directly from the Senate was unusual as well. And for the first time in more than three decades, one candidate threw off the limits imposed on those who accept federal financing in the general election.

To help students of politics make sense of the 2008 general election, in early December 2008 the Annenberg Public Policy Center and its FactCheck.org organized two days of presentations by those responsible for the campaign. The first, involving the McCain and Obama campaign managers, occurred December 5, 2008 at the Annenberg School for Communication of the University of Pennsylvania in Philadelphia. A week later, the second focused on the work of the two major parties and the major Democratic and Republican 527s. This gathering was held at the Newseum in Washington, D.C., December 12, 2008. We have edited the material from these two days for clarity. Inside the back cover of the book is an edited video digest of the segments of the debriefing involving the players in the Obama and McCain campaigns.

Annenberg researchers Jackie Dunn, Karen Riley, and Ken Winneg played a central role in organizing the Philadelphia debriefing. Brooks Jackson and our FactCheck.org staff put together the debriefing in D.C. We join in thanking the debriefing participants for making it possible for us to share their accounts of the 2008 general election with you.

Notes

1. http://www.archives.gov/federal-register/electoral-college/2008/popular-vote.html (U.S. National Archives and Records Administration Office of the Federal Register Website).

2. Ron Suskind, "Change: How Eras End, and Begin," *New York Times Magazine*, November 16, 2006, 55.

The National Annenberg Election Survey

Ken Winneg

In existence since 2000, the National Annenberg Election Survey (NAES), a project of the Annenberg Public Policy Center of the University of Pennsylvania, is the largest public opinion study of the American electorate conducted by a university. The 2008 NAES consisted of two modes of data collection: a nationally representative telephone survey employing a rolling cross-section sampling methodology (RCS) and a five-wave online panel survey.

The 2008 NAES telephone survey began on December 17, 2007 and concluded on November 3, 2008. During this time, 57,967 adults in the United States were interviewed by telephone. The online survey was rolled out on October 1, 2007 and the final wave closed on January 31, 2009. In all, 95,464 interviews were conducted in the panel survey. Although the telephone and panel surveys generally consisted of different questions, both surveys measured beliefs, attitudes, intentions, and behaviors relevant to the 2008 presidential campaigns. Because of its rolling cross-section design, the NAES telephone survey permits scholars to study the effects of events that occur in the campaign.

With the RCS method, random samples of respondents are interviewed each day of the presidential campaign period to ensure that the samples are comparable from one day to the next. Daily interviews can thus be used to identify trends and points of change in public reactions to political events as they unfold over the course of the presidential campaign.

The RCS design is a series of repeated cross-sections collected with a rigorous sampling plan. This sampling plan works to ensure that each of the repeated cross-sections is composed of randomly selected members of the population under study. In the case of the NAES, the design is used to gather cross-sections of randomly selected adults in the United States during the presidential campaign. Because the composition of each cross-section is random, researchers can treat the date of interview as a chance event. They can analyze the data as a single cross-section or a time series.

The sample of telephone exchanges called was randomly selected by a computer from a complete list of all active residential exchanges across the country. Within each exchange, random digits were added to form complete telephone numbers, thus permitting access to both listed and unlisted numbers. Within each household, one adult was designated by a random procedure to be the respondent for the survey. The interviewing was conducted by Abt/SRBI (formerly Schulman, Ronca, Bucuvalas, Inc.).

During the general election period (August 2 through November 3, 2008), the average number of interviews conducted each night was 246. During the early primary period (December 17, 2007, through March 10, 2008), the nightly number of interviews averaged about 233. However, during the post-primary, pre-convention period (June 11 through August 1, 2008) the number of interviews conducted declined significantly, averaging 60 interviews per night. The effect is an increase in the variability of the numbers, which therefore makes the over-time trend during that period less reliable.

Items on the NAES telephone instrument included a variety of measures, for example, evaluations of candidates and political figures. As the presidential campaign progresses, it is critical to track evolving opinions of candidates and political figures that are in some way part of the campaign. These evaluations are an underlying component of NAES. NAES items evaluated the presidential candidates and other political figures on a number of dimensions. These included feeling thermometer ratings, which gauge a general impression of respondents' feelings about the candidates. Respondents were asked to rate the candidates on the so-called "feeling thermometers." In 2008, candidates were rated on a scale from zero to 10 points. A zero score meant the feeling toward the candidate was not favorable at all, while a score of 10 meant the feeling toward the candidate was extremely favorable. Respondents could use any number in between, also.

The 2008 Campaign Timeline tracks the major events of the 2008 election. Chart 1 represents the results of the feeling thermometer, illustrating campaign dynamics from the 2008 presidential race beginning in early August, a few weeks before the Democratic National Convention, and continuing to Election Day (August 5–November 4, 2008). Results are aggregated from the daily RCS data. The daily results are then smoothed using a 5-day moving average, meaning that each day represents an average of that day's results plus the 4 days prior to that point in time. Underlying patterns can be obscured by sampling variation. By averaging results across several days, campaign dynamics are detected more easily. The graph was distributed to participants at the APPC debriefing in December 2008.

CHART 1. CANDIDATE FAVORABILITY, AUGUST 5–NOVEMBER 4, 2008

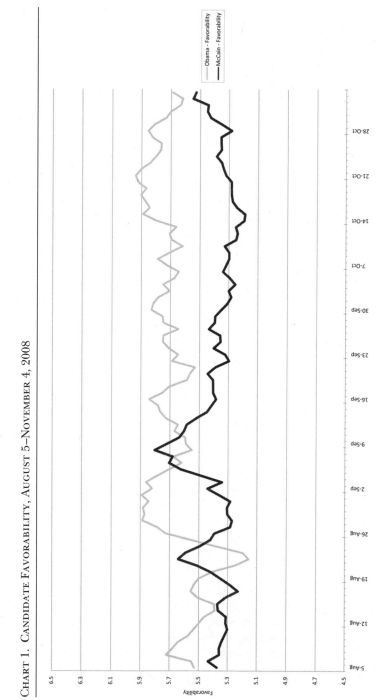

2008 Presidential Campaign Timeline
(prepared by Jacqueline Dunn)

Date	Event
1/3	Mike Huckabee and Barack Obama win Iowa caucuses; Chris Dodd and Joe Biden withdraw from race
1/5	Democratic and Republican Debates in Manchester, New Hampshire (ABC News/Facebook); Mitt Romney wins Wyoming caucus
1/6	Republican Debate in Milford, New Hampshire (FOX)
1/7	California makes mail-in ballots available to voters for its February 5 primary; Hillary Clinton cries at campaign event in New Hampshire
1/8	Clinton and John McCain win New Hampshire primaries
1/10	Republican Debate in Myrtle Beach, South Carolina (FOX); Bill Richardson withdraws from race
1/9–14	Race becomes issue in Democratic primary
1/15	Clinton and Romney win Michigan primary; Democratic Debate in Las Vegas, Nevada
1/19	McCain wins South Carolina primary; Clinton and Romney win Nevada caucuses; Duncan Hunter withdraws from race
1/21	Democratic Debate in Myrtle Beach, South Carolina (CNN)
1/22	Fred Thompson withdraws from race
1/24	Republican Debate in Boca Raton, Florida (MSNBC)
1/25	Dennis Kucinich withdraws from race
1/26	Obama wins South Carolina primary; Bill Clinton sparks criticism by likening Obama's victory to Jesse Jackson's S.C. victories in '84 and '88
1/28	Sen. Edward Kennedy endorses Barack Obama, one day after Caroline Kennedy's endorsement; Bush delivers final State of the Union address
1/29	Clinton and McCain win Florida primaries, no delegates are awarded on Democratic side
1/30	Republican Debate in Simi Valley, California (CNN); Giuliani and Edwards drop out of race; Giuliani immediately endorses McCain
1/31	Democratic Debate in Los Angeles, California (CNN)
2/3	Romney wins Maine caucus
2/5	Super Tuesday—Clinton and Obama essentially split delegates. Obama wins more states (13 for Obama, 9 for Clinton). McCain wins big states (9), Huckabee wins a number of southern states (5)

2/7	Romney withdraws from race during Conservative Political Action Conference; DNC discusses possibility of revote for Michigan and Florida
2/9	Obama wins Louisiana primary and Washington and Nebraska caucuses; Huckabee wins Louisiana primary and Kansas caucus
2/10	Obama wins Maine caucus; Clinton campaign manager Patti Solis Doyle resigns and is replaced by Maggie Williams
2/12	Obama and McCain sweep Chesapeake/Potomac primaries— Maryland, District of Columbia, and Virginia
2/18	Michelle Obama says, "For the first time in my adult life I am proud of my country because it feels like hope is making a comeback" in Milwaukee, Wisconsin; she then says, "For the first time in my adult lifetime, I'm really proud of my country, and not just because Barack has done well, but because I think people are hungry for change" in Madison, Wisconsin
2/19	Obama wins Wisconsin and Hawaii primaries; McCain wins Wisconsin and Washington primaries
2/20	Teamsters Union endorses Obama
2/20–21	*New York Times* publishes article implying that McCain had an inappropriate relationship with lobbyist Vicki Iseman in 2000
2/21	Democratic Debate in Austin, Texas (CNN-Univision)
2/24	Ralph Nader announces his candidacy on *Meet the Press*
2/26	Democratic Debate in Cleveland, Ohio (MSNBC)
2/29	Clinton "3 a.m." ad is released, suggesting her readiness to lead and Obama's inexperience
3/4	Clinton wins Ohio, Texas, and Rhode Island primaries; Obama wins Texas caucuses and Vermont primary; McCain wins Texas, Ohio, Vermont, and Rhode Island and secures Republican nomination; Huckabee withdraws from race
3/5	President Bush endorses McCain one day after McCain clinches nomination
3/8	Obama wins Wyoming caucus
3/11	Obama wins Mississippi primary and Texas caucus
3/11	Geraldine Ferraro, former representative and VP candidate, now working on Clinton campaign as a fundraiser, makes comment attributing Obama's success in the primaries to his race
3/12	Ferraro resigns from Clinton campaign; Gov. Eliot Spitzer—a Clinton superdelegate—resigns as governor of New York after admitting to having sex with a prostitute
3/14	Obama's links to his pastor, Jeremiah Wright, are highlighted

in video clips showing Rev. Wright making derogatory remarks about the U.S. The clips are widely shown on broadcast, cable, and Internet

3/18   Obama makes speech addressing Wright's comments and the issue of race at the National Constitution Center in Philadelphia, Pennsylvania; McCain, in Iraq, mistakenly says that the Shia Iranian government is supporting the Sunni al Qaeda; Obama attacks McCain over gaffe; Clinton releases thousands of records detailing her schedule as first lady, meant to highlight her experience

3/24   Clinton accused of embellishing a story about encountering sniper fire on a trip she took as first lady to Kosovo in 1996. Video footage showed no evidence of sniper fire. Clinton said, "If I misspoke . . . it was a misstatement." Her staff says she misremembered the event

4/4   Hillary Clinton and Bill Clinton's tax returns from 2000–2006 are released

4/6   Obama makes a speech at a closed-door fundraising event in San Francisco and says, "So it's not surprising then that they get bitter, they cling to guns or religion or antipathy to people who aren't like them or anti-immigrant sentiment or anti-trade sentiment as a way to explain their frustrations"; Clinton chief pollster Mark Penn is replaced by Geoffrey Garin

4/12   Clinton criticizes Obama's "bitter" remarks. Obama tries to clarify the remarks, acknowledging that in difficult times people turn to something they can count on

4/13   Clinton and Obama attend Compassion Forum at Messiah College in Pennsylvania

4/15   McCain proposes gas tax holiday

4/16   Democratic Debate in Philadelphia, Pennsylvania (ABC)

4/22   Clinton wins Pennsylvania primary

4/25   Rev. Jeremiah Wright appears on *Bill Moyers Journal*

4/27   Wright speaks at NAACP meeting

4/28   Wright gives a controversial speech at National Press Club in Washington

4/29   Obama denounces Wright after Press Club Talk; on *ABC Good Morning America* Clinton says U.S. could "totally obliterate" Iran

4/30   Clinton appears on *O'Reilly Factor*

5/3   Obama wins Guam primary

5/4   Obama appears on *Meet the Press*. Attacks Clinton over statement she made about "obliterating" Iran if it attacks Israel with nuclear weapons

5/6	Obama wins North Carolina primary; Clinton wins Indiana primary
5/8	Clinton says "Sen. Obama's support among working, hard-working Americans, white Americans is weakening" to *USA Today*
5/13	Clinton wins West Virginia primary
5/14	John Edwards and National Abortion Rights Action League (NARAL) endorse Obama
5/16	California Supreme Court rules 4–3 to strike down state ban on same-sex marriage
5/20	Clinton wins Kentucky primary; Obama wins Oregon primary and claims a majority of committed delegates; Ted Kennedy diagnosed with brain tumor
5/22	McCain denounces and rejects endorsement by Pastor John Hagee after Hagee's comments surface comparing Hitler to a "hunter" sent by G-d to force the Jews back to the promised land
5/23	McCain rejects endorsement by Rev. Rod Parsley who had made negative comments about Islam; Clinton criticized for remark about waiting until the end of primary season to withdraw from the race by evoking her husband's 1992 campaign and Robert Kennedy's assassination at the end of the primary season, June 4, 1968; McCain health records made available for limited scrutiny by press
5/25	Bob Barr wins Libertarian Party nomination
5/27	Obama wins Idaho primary
5/29	Obama releases one page letter from doctor summarizing health
6/1	Clinton wins Puerto Rico primary
6/3	Clinton wins New Mexico and South Dakota primaries; Obama claims enough delegates to become party nominee at the convention; Clinton does not concede
6/4	Obama appoints vice presidential election committee
6/7	Clinton suspends her campaign and throws support behind Obama; Gasoline prices reach a national average of $4.00 per gallon
6/11	Jim Johnson resigns as head of vice presidential vetting team after criticism about his ties to failed mortgage companies and special interests
6/12	Obama campaign launches FightTheSmears.org, a website that will fight back against false rumors about Obama, his campaign, and his family; U.S. Supreme Court rules in controversial 5–4 decision that detainees at Guantanamo Bay

	would be allowed to challenge their detention in federal court
6/15	Obama gives Father's Day speech
6/16	Obama campaign hires Patti Solis Doyle, former Hillary Clinton presidential campaign manager, as chief of staff for Obama's vice presidential nominee
6/17	Al Gore endorses Obama
6/19	Obama announces he will not participate in the public financing system for presidential campaigns
6/24	Bill Clinton announces his support for Obama
6/27	Hillary Clinton announces she will begin campaigning for Obama
7/2	McCain shakes up campaign staff: Steve Schmidt will have full operational control
7/12	Cynthia McKinney nominated for Green Party; McCain wins Nebraska caucus
7/15	*New Yorker* Obama cover sparks controversy
7/17	Obama embarks on world tour
7/18	McCain "Troops Funding" ad airs with claim that Obama canceled visit to troops in Germany
7/19	Obama world tour—Afghanistan
7/21	Obama world tour—Iraq, Jordan
7/23	Obama world tour—Jerusalem, West Bank
7/24	Obama makes speech in Berlin, "A world that stands as one"
7/25	Obama world tour—France
7/26	Obama world tour—ends in Britain
7/30	McCain "Celeb" ad airs, compares Obama to Britney Spears and Paris Hilton; Obama responds with "The Low Road" ad
7/31	Obama makes dollar bill comment in Springfield, Missouri, arguing McCain will say "he doesn't look like all those other presidents on the dollar bills . . ."; McCain campaign says Obama is "playing the race card"
8/3	Bill Clinton gives first interview since Hillary loses primaries—"I am not a racist"; "One can argue no one is ever ready to be president"
8/8	John Edwards admits affair with filmmaker Rielle Hunter
8/16	Saddleback Forum in Lake Forest, California—joint appearance by McCain and Obama
8/21	McCain refers question of how many houses he owns to staff
8/23	Obama announces Joe Biden as his running mate
8/25	Democratic National Convention—Michelle Obama speaks
8/26	Democratic National Convention—Hillary Clinton speaks
8/27	Obama is officially nominated for president by the Demo-

cratic Party. Democratic National Convention—Bill Clinton, Joe Biden speak

8/28   Democratic National Convention—Obama receives nomination, speech

8/29   McCain announces Sarah Palin as his running mate

9/1   Republican National Convention—Laura Bush and Cindy McCain speak; Bristol Palin pregnancy announced

9/2   Republican National Convention—Fred Thompson and Joe Lieberman speak

9/3   Republican National Convention—Rudy Giuliani and Sarah Palin speak, McCain officially nominated for president by the Republican Party

9/7   Government seizes Fannie Mae and Freddie Mac, twin mortgage buyers

9/10   Obama makes "Lipstick on a pig" comment in Lebanon, Virginia

9/11   Palin's interview with CBS's Charlie Gibson airs

9/15   Lehman Bros. files for bankruptcy protection

9/16   Bank of America buys Merrill Lynch for $50 million after government rejects aid package

9/17   Government bails out AIG

9/24   McCain announces he is "suspending his campaign" to return to Washington and work on bailout, debate up in air; Obama says president can multitask; Part I of Palin's interview with CBS's Katie Couric airs

9/25   Part II of Palin's interview with Couric airs

9/26   First Presidential Debate in Oxford, Mississippi

9/28   Dow Jones loses 777 points, largest single-day loss in its history

9/29   House rejects initial bailout plan; Dow Jones drops 7%

10/1   Senate adds earmarks, repurposes bailout plan for $700 billion, passes by wide margin

10/2   Vice Presidential Debate in St. Louis, Missouri; McCain pulls out of Michigan

10/3   Bailout plan approved

10/4   Palin says Obama "pals around with terrorists" (Ayers)

10/7   Second Presidential Debate in Nashville, Tennessee

10/11   Rep. John Lewis (D-Ga.) likens McCain/Palin campaign to that of segregationist George Wallace

10/13   McCain "Comeback" speech in Virginia Beach; U.S. investing $250 billion in the banking industry

10/14   Jesse Jackson "Israel" comment breaks in news, blogs; McCain releases new fiscal policies

10/15	Third Presidential Debate in Hempstead, New York
10/16	McCain and Obama speak at Al Smith dinner
10/18	Palin appears on *Saturday Night Live*
10/19	Colin Powell endorses Obama on *Meet the Press*
10/21	RNC states that it spent $150,000 on Sarah Palin's wardrobe
10/27	Sen. Ted Stephens (R-Ak.) is found guilty of failing to report more than $250,000 in gifts
10/29	Obama airs 30-minute spot on prime-time television on several networks
11/1	McCain appears on *Saturday Night Live*
11/4	Election Day: Obama is elected 44th President of the United States

The Vice Presidential Campaign

Nicolle Wallace

Nicolle Wallace *served as a senior advisor to the McCain-Palin campaign from May to November 2008. Prior to joining the McCain campaign, she worked as a political analyst at CBS News. She served as an assistant to President George W. Bush, as director of communications for the White House from January 2005 to June 2006, as communications director for President Bush's 2004 reelection campaign, and as special assistant to the president and director of media affairs at the White House, where she oversaw regional press strategy and outreach. Wallace was Florida Governor Jeb Bush's press secretary in 1999 and served California's Assembly Republican Caucus from 1997 to 1998.*

Our selection of Governor Sarah Palin was like a whirlwind romance. It was the highest highs of the campaign for us, as well as some of the greatest challenges. What she faced from the media were some of the most wrenching news cycles for us as a campaign.

I'll start at her selection. We made history in the fact that the identity of John McCain's running mate was the first secret the McCain campaign actually kept. I went back and looked at what was happening in the campaign at the time that we made the decision. A lot of people forget that the top domestic issue, at least in the press, was the price of energy, gas prices. People were driving all over. People were stealing gas. We were running on the Lexington Project, which was John McCain's initiative to create a path toward true energy independence in America.

We also faced the strategic imperative of needing to win the support of some of Senator Hillary Clinton's former supporters. We were very eager to win over women voters. We were also running in a party that was deeply unpopular and distrusted. [As a result] it was a strategic imperative and, I think, personally important to John McCain to remind voters of his record of standing up against entrenched special interests and, probably more important, his own party.

He sought a running mate who had done some of the same things that he had done, had stood up to special interests, had stood up to her own party, had taken a stand against corruption and was a doer and a player on the national energy scene.

There have been a lot of stories told about planes flying out of Alaska in the middle of the night. I think she flew on one of them to [Senator McCain's home in] Sedona [Arizona]. She met with Steve [Schmidt] and Mark Salter and Senator McCain and his wife. The nominee and her family were then transported to a very dingy hotel in Youngstown, Ohio. In the morning we were looking out the windows to see if any press had figured out where we were. They still didn't know who our nominee was. Our joke was "they'll never suspect we're here. The campaign staff would never stay in a place like this."

When they arrived the night before her announcement, the children [in her family] were unaware that their mother had been selected. The staff had begun work on his announcement speech. And Steve informed the kids that their mother had been selected as the [Republican] vice presidential nominee.

I think from the moment that her announcement speech was deliv-

Nicolle Wallace

ered to the moment that her convention speech was delivered would be phase one of the Palin candidacy. Out of the blocks we were getting questions from mainstream news organizations about the maternity and paternity of her 12-week infant son Trig. Within 48 hours of her announcement speech, she was forced to reveal that her 17-year-old daughter was five months pregnant to, frankly, prove that the three-month-old infant who is her child had not been born to her daughter. It was one of the most stunning periods of earned media interaction I think any of us had probably ever experienced. Despite that, I think she gave two extraordinary performances, both in her announcement speech, where she certainly captured the imagination of our party and excited the Republican base and Republican supporters and even our press in a way they hadn't been before that point.

Then in the period leading up to her convention there were 742 stories about how she hadn't been vetted. There were over 500 blogs about the maternity of her infant. And there were a couple of tabloid stories about whether she'd been faithful. It was an extraordinary period in which the governor of Alaska prepared for and delivered one of the best convention speeches certainly by any candidate at the top or in the second spot of the ticket in the Republican Party. In the Palin campaign, we viewed that as one period.

Her convention speech was drafted by the same brilliant speech writer who worked on her announcement speech. The chemistry between Matt Scully and Sarah Palin was like the relationship of Mark Salter and John McCain. They finished each other's sentences. The line [from the convention speech] that everyone replays that I think came to define Sarah Palin in the early part of that campaign was her line "pundits and reporters will say what they will. I'm not going to Washington to curry their good favor. I'm going to serve the American people." In retrospect that was like waving a red flag. We paid for that every day for the next 66 days.

But I think that it also cemented her. She had a connection with the voters, certainly with Republican supporters. She brought in new supporters because she made clear from go that she was there for them. I think that's what she carved out in that first introduction to the convention and to the voters. I think that that stayed with her and I think it will stay with her.

A lot has been said about the media rollout, the decision to do high stakes network interviews. Anyone who works on a campaign certainly looks at any event that doesn't serve a candidate well and wishes they could pull it back and have not done it. The campaign never thought twice, though, about having Sarah Palin do high profile interviews. She was picked to be a messenger for John McCain's candidacy, his cause, what he was fighting for. She remained for much of the campaign the most effective voice at speaking to people's economic angst. She'd been through it before. I think she talked in her debate about how when they had their first child, she and Todd didn't have health insurance. This wasn't someone who [merely] studied America's health care crisis. This was someone who lived it.

We consider her first three interviews the rollout. The first one was Charlie Gibson. The second was Sean Hannity. And the third was the much noted, replayed, and spoofed Katie Couric interview. There was a lot of pressure to do a Sunday show. But she had just said, "I'm not going to Washington to curry the favor of the pundits and insiders." I can't remember giving serious consideration to doing a Sunday show. But it seems so clear now that that would have been a mistake. There was a lot of pressure to do a news magazine, a *60 Minutes*.

We chose Charlie Gibson because the goal always was to have as many eyeballs as possible see everything she said and did. Since she was such a phenomenon at our convention, [we knew that] there would be no local media that were only seen in a single market. Everything she did and said would be amplified by the national media. Every radio interview she did ended up [featured] on network television.

She did over two hours of on-air interviews with Charlie Gibson on her first and only trip back to Alaska I guess a week after the convention, the—the Friday and Saturday or Thursday and Friday after the convention.

We felt that she did great. She I think had very confident strong answers to every single question except the definitional question about what the Bush doctrine was. There was a little bit of focus on it. Then it certainly became clear that a lot of people in the Bush administration had different answers to what exactly is the Bush doctrine. She then rolled into a Sean Hannity interview.

None of those really got the attention that her stumbles in the first part of the Katie Couric interview did. I spent a long time thinking about why that was. When someone is unknown, there's a hunger for information and [an eagerness] to evaluate her competence, and strengths and weaknesses [are exaggerated].

She was probably ill served by the timing of that interview. It came in the middle of 17 or 20 bilateral meetings with foreign leaders, obviously the first in her career. And she sat down the day after the bailout legislation was first proposed on the Hill, [legislation that elicited] very political and very intense reactions on both sides. She was kind of plopped down in the middle of it.

After that she did a second interview with Katie Couric that we considered putting off or having her not do. But I think her style with the media was to take them on and to fight and to make her best case not for herself but for John McCain and for the campaign.

Among the good things she did [was becoming] very engaged with her traveling press. She found them irresistible. [She'd] go back and—and greet them. She was accessible to them. She did a ton of radio. You can always look back, certainly when you come up short, and reexamine the rollout or reexamine the announcement. But when we look at the Palin rollout, we looked at it as her announcement in Ohio, which was certainly the best-kept secret of the McCain campaign and one of our most dramatic moments, and the convention speech. John McCain could not have been more proud of her on that night.

Afterward, he said, "She did great. You know, that was so great." I said, "Yeah, and her teleprompter wasn't working properly. It couldn't stop on a dime. So when there was an applause line, it didn't stop in time." (She lost the first two lines, which was really only about six words. But when you're a staffer, you hold your breath.) And I said to him, "Yeah, she did great. And the prompter didn't work. She didn't have the first two lines."

He said, "Oh, god, we're screwed if that happens to me." [So she gave] two extraordinary speeches and a very strong performance with Charlie Gibson and Sean Hannity and, unfortunately, a performance that I think she felt could have been much better in the first part of that Katie Couric interview. It was what it was. . . .

It's always about risk and reward. We took some risks in that rollout strategy. In some ways we didn't have a lot to lose. We were behind eight or nine by the last day of your [the Democratic] convention and we went for it. I'm sure there are things we did wrong and things we could have done better but that was the rollout strategy as we envisioned it and as it was executed.

Mark D. Wallace

Ambassador Mark D. Wallace serves as president of United Against Nuclear Iran, a bipartisan foreign policy coalition. During the 2008 presidential campaign, Wallace led the preparation of Governor Sarah Palin in anticipation of the October 2, 2008, vice presidential debate. Previously, he served as U.S. Ambassador to the United Nations, Representative for UN Management and Reform, and in a variety of government, political, and private sector posts. In the Department of Homeland Security, Wallace was principal legal advisor to the Bureau of Immigration and Customs Enforcement and to the Bureau of Immigration and Citizenship Services. During the 2004 presidential campaign, Wallace served as the Bush-Cheney '04 deputy campaign manager and as the campaign's lead liaison to the Republican National Convention and its representative in debate negotiations.

After the three major interviews that launched her, we began focusing on her debate preparations. Any candidate coming to a debate has life experiences and professional experiences. Otherwise, they wouldn't be there. And there was something great about the fact that Sarah Palin [was] from Wasilla, Alaska. Both literally and figuratively very, very far away from Washington. There was something great about talking to a politician who had enormous skill and talent and rose from being on the PTA to the city council to the city mayor to the governor of the state and ultimately to being the vice presidential nominee of the Republican Party. That's part of who she was. And a lot of people identified with her for those reasons.

Nicolle touched on one already. In our discussions we talked about health care at one point. The Palin family didn't have health care insurance for a significant time. They were grappling with insuring their family. I would imagine not many major candidates have gone through that experience. So she could identify with many Americans around the country in ways perhaps that other candidates had not. But, it's perhaps a statement of the obvious, a candidate with the life experience of Sarah Palin probably was not dealing with the intricacies of NATO on a daily basis.

The greatness of our political system is that we can have candidates who have an incredible understanding of both local and state politics that is removed from Washington. [But their experiences do not necessarily ensure that they will be familiar with] the intricacies of NATO. When Senator Obama was working in Chicago and doing an incredibly good job I would imagine that he did not focus on the intricacies of NATO. But I don't know that.

I think she was a very good retail politician. We've seen that on the stump. She was compelling. She [also] was voracious about wanting to learn. A small group of us met with her on the campaign trail as we went from hotel to hotel. It was difficult to carve in time to prepare her for her debate because of the inordinate attention being focused on her. Ultimately the prep process moved to Sedona with a smaller group. There the discussion was even more intensive. I think she thrived there. The stakes of the debate were obviously very high. When you look at the history of vice presidential debates, they typically have not moved numbers and not commanded enormous viewership.

The viewership of the vice presidential debate was higher than for any of the presidential debates. I think there was a combination of the newness of Governor Palin and the incredible experience and talent of Sen-

Mark Wallace

ator Biden on the other side, a very compelling matchup, if you will. Some people were probably expecting, as they would in an auto race, some were looking for crashes. The result was incredible viewership. In Governor Palin, we had a compelling new figure on the stage and the stakes were quite high [as a result]. As I think back, I don't believe there's anything comparable in vice presidential debates historically.

If you look at the vice presidential debate with vice president Cheney, we had I think about a nine point lead in 2004 in the Bush/Kerry race. That lead evaporated after the president's first debate with Senator Kerry. So we learned that the stakes were very high. We were startled at the drop after that first debate. After the first presidential debate in 2008 the numbers did not move dramatically one way or the other. We were a little behind. The stakes [of the vice presidential debate] were high. I think Governor Palin really rose to the occasion and performed incredibly well. I will also say that I think that Senator Biden did as well. You had two incredibly talented candidates giving their best performances in that debate. And I think it was compelling.

After that debate process, I think that she even had a newfound confidence, because it was a big deal. Seventy million viewers watched that vice presidential debate. It was a big deal. I think she really found her mojo after the vice presidential debate. We saw crowds for Governor Palin that were phenomenal. In an Orlando event before the debate there was an enormous crowd. . . . One of our local events team gave the number, 90,000 people. I said, "We're not putting that out. We're immediately going to be attacked. We're going to look like fools if you say 90,000 people." And he said, "No, the police chief is saying 60,000 to 90,000 people." I said, "Let me hear from the police chief. Let them say that because [Obama advisor David] Plouffe is going to attack us if overstate the numbers—"

NICOLLE WALLACE:

No, [Obama representative Bill] Burton would have attacked it.

MARK WALLACE:

Burton would have given us a hard time. But the police chief literally said 90,000. They ultimately released something above 60,000 people. It was a phenomenal retail event. She thrived in that atmosphere. She's incredibly strong in the retail politics of communicating on the stump. People love her. Her talent is obvious. And I think that people can identify with the fact that she is from Wasilla. . . .

One of the press accounts said that she was going rogue and deviating from Senator McCain's message at times. It was parodied. We didn't spend a lot of time knocking that down because I think it was part of her brand, frankly. We viewed it as a bonus. John McCain, known as a maverick, had selected somebody else who was willing to speak her mind and differ and be compelling in other ways. I think there was a lot of inside baseball discussion at that time about this going-rogue phenomenon

She did other [forms of] press such as Rush Limbaugh, types of media that garnered a lot of attention but were not satisfying to the mainstream press. She was out there more than conventional wisdom would suggest.

The pick [of Governor Palin] in and of itself was a very consequential pick in terms of the dynamic of the race. I do believe [however] that Senator McCain could have had Hercules on the ticket and he probably would not have won given some of the dynamic. And I think any attempt to portray that she somehow dragged Senator McCain down is inaccurate. I think she was consequential in many great ways.

JOEL BENENSON:

Nicolle, you mentioned that you thought you'd waved a red flag at the press with the line in the speech. But you also deviated from history in that over the past 40 years no vice presidential candidate had gone more than 10 days without having a traditional press conference. You folks chose not to do that. Do you think that that was the red flag that got them going more than one line in the VP speech?

NICOLLE WALLACE:

We'd had a roller coaster ride with the press. Because of McCain's long history of accessibility we'd had a pretty drawn out deliberation with the press over access to him. The press that traveled with her didn't agitate for that because she eventually started coming back [to talk with reporters]. I think an interview strategy is a pretty accepted rollout, particularly for somebody new on the scene.

Frankly, we looked at some of the things you had done post-announcement. I think a press conference is often the last piece when you're introducing someone new and huge. You do some interviews where you can interact and define yourself one-on-one. When you work in campaigns, you do a lot of self-flagellation. But not a single person beat themselves up about not getting to a full-scale press conference.

DAVID PLOUFFE:

I'm wondering if the—"Can I call you Joe" thing was a strategy of the debate.

MARK WALLACE:

That's a good question. I'll tell one story. I don't like talking about the intricacies of the prep. I think it's inappropriate to do that. But I was standing in the wings with Governor Palin and she said, "Should I ask to call him—Joe or Senator Biden?" I think there was a desire, if she was going to personalize it, to be polite and ask permission. He's a sitting senator, somebody to be respected. Although there's a lot of speculation about the decision to do that, there was no tactic about that decision. It was really a comfort thing for her.

ANITA DUNN:

I know from our own vice presidential process the challenge of getting ready for very different kinds of VP candidates with the secret very tightly kept within campaigns and not really being able to think through the different approaches and communication strategies. But I am wondering, given the fact that she was a woman—whether you felt having a little more time to think through the gender issues, particularly having watched the Clinton primary campaign, is something you feel you would have benefited from?

NICOLLE WALLACE:

I met her for the first time at 10:00 p.m. Matt Scully, the speech writer who's a brilliant speech writer in his day job, [is] in his part-time job an animal rights activist. He went in there and wrote a speech for the wolf-killing moose hunter. No one had any time to think about much of anything. Steve opened the door and said, "Hand me your BlackBerry. Meet our nominee." And it was, (CLAP) "write a speech, get on a plane, go to Minneapolis."

I think we were very cognizant, though, of presenting her first and foremost as ready. We had 64 days to convince the American people that she was ready to step into the presidency. And I'm sure you guys feel the same way. At the top of a campaign there are about five people, four people. People would say, "Who's out with McCain? I'm out with Palin. Where are you?" All of us had nine jobs. Sure, [were there time] that would have been ideal.

ANITA DUNN:

I'm just curious.

NICOLLE WALLACE:

Yeah.

ANITA DUNN:

I was actually giving you the opportunity to go negative—

NICOLLE WALLACE:

Yeah.

ANITA DUNN:

—on your management as—

NICOLLE WALLACE:

(LAUGHTER). No, no, no. We were all—we were all—

MARK WALLACE:

In our prep, there was one moment where we had a small—relatively small group that was working on prepping her. I looked around the room and it was all a bunch of dudes at one point.

NICOLLE WALLACE:

Yeah.

MARK WALLACE:

And I said, hey, what's wrong with this picture? We need a woman's presence. It was important to do that. But it was also important in that prep that we not make it about prepping a woman but about prepping the vice president. It was very important to show her readiness given both her age and her gender because we were breaking new ground. But we had to show that there really was no difference. And I think that's the way she wanted it, frankly.

ANITA DUNN:

In our party obviously we have the advantage of Emily's List, which has done an enormous amount of research over the years into women running for office.

MARK WALLACE:

We don't have that.

NICOLLE WALLACE:

We have Bill [McInturff]. We were not unaware—of this—

ANITA DUNN:

No, I know. But I'm—but I'm just saying the—the fact is it's not the same yet.

NICOLLE WALLACE:

Right.

ANITA DUNN:

Just the same as some of the issues we had with our nominee.

NICOLLE WALLACE:

Absolutely. Absolutely.

MARK WALLACE:

Sure.

ANITA DUNN:

She's a great performer—

NICOLLE WALLACE:

Yeah.

ANITA DUNN:

—and in her rollout and in her convention speech and in the debate she performed extremely well. But did you feel that even that extra 24 hours could have helped prepare a little force on the backlash—

NICOLLE WALLACE:

No doubt.

ANITA DUNN:

—because your campaign very openly argued that it was a gender backlash as much as an elitist backlash. And none of you mentioned that in your presentations.

NICOLLE WALLACE:

Absolutely.

ANITA DUNN:

But you were saying that—

NICOLLE WALLACE:

We argued anything that gets through the news cycle.

MARK WALLACE:

From a debate perspective, one of the things that we did consider was how Senator Biden would deal with some of the issues of the day. Remember, you're thinking about an hour and a half debate. In that format, you're generally looking at 18 questions, maybe a little bit more, a little bit less. You know the likely subject matter that will come up.

The policy questions that were probably the most dominant were different from the crazy press focus in some ways on Governor Palin. My own prediction was that Senator Biden was a gentleman and on top of being a gentleman, it would be very, very perilous for him to engage in that way, so he would stay hands off completely on the subject. From a strategic perspective, that was the bet. I think it was a pretty safe bet, frankly. It was good advice.

NICOLLE WALLACE:

It had a life of its own. I think Charlie Gibson was somewhat traumatized by the horrible round of press that he got. The campaign decided in the first 72 hours that we would not discuss hair, makeup, clothes, appearances because we had never seen a male candidate address such questions.

Workouts were different. You were pretty open. So she went running in front of the camera. She did speak about being a working mom and having kids on the trail, and we would have loved to have had her speak about it more. We understood from [McCain pollster] Bill [McInturff] that from the middle of September on the economy was the first, second, third, fourth, and fifth concern of women.

Two very smart women came with her. One was Meg Stapleton who was a press aide in Alaska. The other was Kris Perry who worked alongside Mark in the debate prep. Some of it was her wanting to stay true to what had always been her political identity.

MARK WALLACE:

You're obviously treading new ground when you have a mom who has young children on the campaign. What is the level of intrusion? What is the level of access? Those were daily difficult discussions. In retrospect, if I would have changed something on the campaign, I would have tried to think through some of those things because it has an effect on the family, an effect on young children. In retrospect, I think that should be thought out more. There was no manual, a 44-year-old mom, young kids, now vice presidential nominee—

NICOLLE WALLACE:

On the bus. (LAUGHTER)

MARK WALLACE:

—on the bus.

DAVID AXELROD:

This is the first time I've heard Bill [McInturff] referred to as the corollary to Emily's List. Given what you said, Nicolle, about the fact that she was sitting down with world leaders for the first time, she was having to handle these macroeconomic issues—in a way she hadn't before. I get what you're saying. I understood completely what her appeal was. I think we all did. But one of the things that Obama thought about when he picked his VP candidate was, having gone through the maelstrom of being introduced into the national political scene in the way he was, he understood the pressures that would be placed on a candidate. And one of the reasons he chose Senator Biden was because Biden was familiar with the track. He had been through that. He knew that it was not unfamiliar turf to him and he certainly knew these issues. In retrospect, was the tradeoff a good tradeoff? That's the first question. And the second one is, how much do you think Tina Fey impacted public perceptions of Palin?

NICOLLE WALLACE:

I spoke to a reporter we all know and love last night for a long time. He asked me the same question. The question is presented as though curtain number two was the ideal. I disagree with the notion that we didn't have good choices. We had very good choices. We'd had a robust primary. [Former Massachusetts governor] Mitt Romney and [current Minnesota governor] Tim Pawlenty were out there. But we were down nine. We needed a game changer. I don't know what other game changer option there was for us. Had energy prices remained the top domestic issue, it's possible it could have turned out differently. But the arc of events took us to a global economic crisis. And the first time she was asked about it [in the Couric interview], she left an impression of not understanding the complexity of the bailout. I think it's pretty obvious that as events changed they made her candidacy more challenging in some regards. I think she would acknowledge that. But it's hard to examine curtain number two or three and say that would have worked out so much better.

Tina Fey. I actually think as many people saw Tina Fey as saw the actual Couric interview. I think it was seeing the filtering in a couple questions. "I have to get back to you," which then became "Can I have a lifeline?" I hope I get one, one day in my career. Maybe today. They were two halves of a whole that became a competence narrative that she had to deal with.

And I think one of the most attractive things about her [Governor Palin] and I said this to her after the Gibson interview is that although she didn't answer every question perfectly the way your candidate would have, she fought. That's what people loved. She fought her way through the whole campaign. With some of these issues even with all of her fight, she still couldn't make the case that the global economic meltdown was something she could be conversant on in the 20 minutes she had to think about it before a network interview.

MARK WALLACE:

I would challenge the premise of one part of your question a little bit. We had more compressed time [than you did with Obama]. So you have a difference there.

But I also think that Senator Obama and Senator McCain, now President-elect Obama, did a very good job ruling things out for one another at times about the appropriateness of the scrutiny. To Senator and now President-elect Obama's credit, I remember he ruled out some of the inquiries on Governor Palin's family.

I am not one to be critical of the press. They're our friends. [But a] number of our friends approached me and said it's not really her baby—

NICOLLE WALLACE:

Yeah.

JIM MARGOLIS:

I want to play just a little bit further on the experience question because this was a big strategic change for you. Everything had been predicated to that point on McCain being ready. He was the experienced one. We were the ones who were not up to this job. Overnight that shifted with the Palin selection. So clearly that must have been a big part of the conversation internally. Was it this feeling that you just had to have a game changer that was of that magnitude that you could push aside all of that messaging?

NICOLLE WALLACE:

Yes. When you lose, you get to give one-word answers. We needed a game changer. We were at the end of the Democratic convention down eight? Is that about right? Down eight. There were people who would have been more experienced and we could have spent 67 days running on experience, which hadn't worked against you in the primary.

It was a strategy. We weren't sure it was a winning strategy. We had to prioritize and we chose to reinforce energy independence, being a maverick, the courage to go against your own party, picking someone who represents the future of the Republican Party. Her positives outweighed the things that others may have been stronger on experience, certain experience in dealing with global economic issues or foreign policy.

JIM MARGOLIS:

But it was a fundamental change in the campaign's message. It wasn't secondary. This was at the core of the McCain candidacy.

STEVE SCHMIDT:

There are two elements to it. It was our view that after the president-elect returned from his overseas trip we were at a point very, very close to Senator Obama running away with the race. And I had always felt that if we got into a situation where we got down double digits in the month of August, that the race was effectively over. When we made our strategic assumptions in the race, one was that you were going to have a very good convention, he [Senator Obama] was going to give a terrific speech, and that if we entered our convention in a situation where we were down 15 or 16 points, it was lights out.

We also believed at the end of the day that experience was not a message that was going to win the election for us. We believed that in order to win the election or have any chance coming out of the convention, we needed to do a number of different things, some of them contradictory. We needed to get our piece of the change issue. It was a change election and that the experience issue [needed to be cast as] John McCain had the experience to change and to lead reform. So we needed to come out of the convention, into the fall campaign, being able to be a credible messenger on the change and reform issue, number one. Number two, we needed to distance ourselves finally and completely from the administration in a very profound way. We needed to appeal to the middle of the electorate, number three. And number four, we had to excite the base of the party. We had an unexcited party. We needed to do those four things. We never intended to run on experience in the course of the fall campaign. We came out of the convention. We seized a lead in the campaign I think with the reform credential, with the change credential, with the distance from Bush.

Our ballot was tied to the perception "you're four more years of President Bush" or not. When that number went down, our ballot went up. When that number went up, our ballot went down. As I look back on the race, we did everything we could think of. At a strategic level, it was, to analogize it to boxing, about staying on your feet at that point and surviving the round, as the right track number dropped to—

NICOLLE WALLACE:

Four. . . .

STEVE SCHMIDT:

—5 percent. We used to joke "Who would have thought having the right track number at 20 percent would have been the good old days?"

JOEL BENENSON:

In our parlor betting, I believed you needed a game changer, too, but my money was on Lieberman. I know there was a conflict there between the base and the middle. Did you give any thought to the fact that we were in a post-partisan period and picking a Democrat would have sent a very powerful message? Why wasn't he the game changer?

STEVE SCHMIDT:

Without getting into the deliberative process of the senator's decision making on this, I think it is safe to say because of the press reports that Senator Lieberman was under consideration. It would have been an exciting and dynamic pick. I agree with you from an outcome perspective that the effect of that would have been electrifying to the broader electorate. Bill can speak to the consequences of nominating somebody who is not pro-life on the Republican Party number a little bit later.

But we would not have been able to get him nominated through the convention. We knew certainly at a minimum [that there would have] been four states that would have nominated their own vice presidential nominee. We were already in the middle of a truncated convention. Not with hindsight but prospectively said, there's another category five hurricane about to destroy New Orleans on the exact anniversary of Katrina on the night the president's going to speak at the Republican convention.

MARK WALLACE:

That was a great night.

NICOLLE WALLACE:

You always thought you were in the valley in the McCain campaign. But then it got deeper.

MARK WALLACE:

And darker.

STEVE SCHMIDT:

Reporters asked this a lot. I said, "You're writing a great screenplay. It's like an episode from the *West Wing*." The reality is that if we had a floor fight at our convention which had the potential to knock all the speakers out of primetime, it would have been a spectacle for the ages. We believe we would have blown up the Republican Party.

NICOLLE WALLACE:

And we thought about it. (LAUGHTER)

STEVE SCHMIDT:

And we gave it serious consideration. But in the end didn't think it was a survivable event.

BILL MCINTURFF:

My counsel internally was, if we were considering Senator Lieberman, who by the way I think might have been Senator McCain's preference, at a minimum both Senator McCain and Senator Lieberman would have to pledge to serve one term because the only way to nominate him through that convention process would have been a promise that he would never ever try to serve or rerun as a Republican.

You'd have to say, "We're doing a one-term, fix-America bipartisan, solve-our-big-problems, I'm-72-years-old, we're-going to-change-entitlements." You could have run that campaign. One thing that running for president has done for me [which is] different than running all the other big statewide, is these men and women could serve as the American president. It is a different job from any I've ever done before. Take our decision never to talk about Reverend Wright. I said, "If John McCain's going to win, we're going to lose the popular vote by three million votes. There will be an enormous potential for urban violence." Imagine if we had done that and he'd been doing Reverend Wright and trying to actually serve as American president. It would have delegitimized his presidency.

So in the same way, Senator McCain had to make a decision. Could you serve as the American president with a promise never to run again? As you know, it's a fairly weak office. The command that you have is that you have political capital and they should be afraid of you. If you start your office with, "We have this odd partnership and we're leaving in four years"—I think Senator McCain rightfully came to the conclusion you [could not] govern as President.

I believe we would have lost by six points anyway, whoever's the VP. Had we chosen Senator Lieberman, we would have been fighting through October inside our party. That would have been a month's worth of stories about fighting the party. Then we would have lost by six points. We would have lost all these Senate seats and House seats. And Senator McCain would have been blamed for demolishing the Republican Party. That would have been the consequence.

DAVID AXELROD:

Obviously we saw the reports that he was considering potentially going for a one-term option. And we looked at it. At some point here we ought to give a little nod to the American people. We may be more eager to give them a nod today than you guys. The reality is that they're a lot smarter than they get credit for. They think these things through. And they were very cool on this notion of a one-term presidency. I thought it might be appealing because it takes the politics out of it and all that. But our sense was that it was not a lightning strike. It was a self-neutering gesture and would not have worked out well.

BROOKS JACKSON, FACTCHECK.ORG:

One of the things we dealt with through the whole campaign at Fact-Check.org were Internet rumors, first with Obama and then with Sarah Palin, this tsunami of Internet rumors, some true but a lot of them false. I wonder if you thought about this. From a campaign standpoint, what's the takeaway lesson here? How do you, as a candidate, deal with these things?

MARK WALLACE:

Don't let your candidate have access to the Internet.

NICOLLE WALLACE:

Yeah, that was a problem.

BROOKS JACKSON:

Well you didn't have a problem. But—

NICOLLE WALLACE:

No, but she saw everything.

MARK WALLACE:

I think it upset her. I think she should speak to that herself.

BROOKS JACKSON:

My question isn't, "How does the candidate emotionally deal with them?" but "How do you counteract these things?"

NICOLLE WALLACE:

I think a good thing that was done [by the Obama campaign] was Fight TheSmears.org. We thought about that with her. It seemed a little bit me-too-ism. We obviously didn't master it. We were dogged by the

Internet crud on her for all of the first three weeks and much of the last six.

MARK WALLACE:

We had our own fact checking. We had a rapid response teams, set up our own websites. Those are the standard tools and tactics that you employ. I do think that it's harder in a shorter timeframe. I think that we were deluged with all the rumors in a shorter period of time.

When Internet rumors fly around, you have to have them out there long enough so that they're ridiculed as nonsensical for some period of time. President-elect Obama obviously suffered all sorts of crazy things out there. You were very effective in knocking them down. I think you did have the advantage of the longer primary to knock them down.

NICOLLE WALLACE:

It took a while, right.

MARK WALLACE:

It took a while. We didn't have that luxury.

NICOLLE WALLACE:

I will say one thing, though. You have to break the circuit. You have to snap the hardwiring of the crazy left-wing blogs into newsrooms. For us it was MS(NBC). There was an increasingly rapid information flow from the Daily Kos to—sometimes Politico, some of those covering Democratic campaigns into, you know, maybe like a [David] Shuster show or an [Keith] Olbermann show on MS(NBC) into the mainstream media asking us a question. So we figured out how to snap that. We did some of what you did. We called them out on it [and] challenged legitimate reporters to knock down some of the stuff they knew was crap.

One of our lessons of the convention and, frankly, a lot of reporters warned us of this. "I know you've been seeing these things on the Internet. My desk is now asking me about it." We were aware of the urgent need to call out this hardwiring from the left-wing blogs into some of commentary hours. . . . We tried to snap that cycle.

MARK WALLACE:

One difficulty of those Internet rumors was they were all coming at once in a shorter period of time. We were trying to drive a message at that time. It's harder to knock down those rumors in a shorter period of time when you're trying to drive an affirmative message.

Chapter 2

Campaign Management and Field Operations

David Plouffe

__David Plouffe__ is a partner at the firm AKP&D and one of the more experienced and successful strategists in the Democratic Party. As executive director of the Democratic Congressional Campaign Committee from 1999 to 2000, Plouffe led a focused national campaign that moved a record $95 million to House races across the country. Prior to joining the DCCC, Plouffe served as Democratic leader Richard Gephardt's deputy chief of staff. He joined Gephardt after managing the successful campaign to fill Bill Bradley's seat in the U.S. Senate for Bob Torricelli, the most hotly contested Senate race in the 1996 cycle. Plouffe served as campaign director at the Democratic Senatorial Campaign Committee in 1995, joining the DSCC after managing a U.S. Senate race in Delaware in 1994 for Attorney General Charlie Oberly against Senator Bill Roth.

I'd first say this to our friends in the McCain campaign. We went through something for two years that very few people can understand. It's a small fraternity of people who go through the ups and lows in politics. We appreciated being on the battlefield with you.

Our opponents had three extra months we would have liked to have had. We had a compressed five-month period to put together a general election. I'm going to start by talking about some of the big strategy assumptions we made, some of the tactics we employed, some of the bigger decisions we had to make. Some of that will bleed into what Jon has to say.

First of all, the media were fascinated with "can the party be unified?" We simply weren't that concerned about it. We thought that by November 4, and in some cases earlier than that, where the early vote was, we would get 88 to 94 percent of the Democratic vote, depending on the state. If we didn't, we were in big trouble anyway. So we didn't spend a lot of time in the campaign hand wringing about it.

There were still polls on this in September and October; most of them

David Plouffe

were flawed. We just weren't obsessed with it. We just had to take a leap of faith that all would be fine or we were going to be in some difficulty.

So we came out of the primary [season] with some big moments that we focused on. We had the foreign trip. Even though the celebrity ads were interesting, and I agree with Steve, probably ended up leveling off a little bit of the effect of that [trip], I'm convinced it was a huge benefit for us. It was part of the fabric of the campaign. When we did focus groups in the fall, it was still something that came up.

They liked the fact that he did well over there. The speech in Berlin, while ridiculed, was something that people liked. They liked the fact that an American potential president could draw that kind of crowd and have that kind of message. So we focused on the foreign trip, which, of these big things, was maybe the most perilous and the hardest thing to do. We almost went in the fall of '07 but we pulled that trip back at the very end. It was really hard to do and so we were thrilled with how it got executed.

Then there was the VP selection, the convention, and the three debates. Some of the [McCain] ads on celebrity were clever. You did a very good job of pushing that. Our belief was, there were moments in the campaign that were going to be a natural antidote to that, the selection of the vice president, the nomination speech, the presidential debates. Particularly, if he acquitted himself well, [these events] would run counter to the notion that we were all hat and no cattle.

So I thought it was a clever tactic, and there's no doubt that it provided you some momentum and energy. But we weren't that concerned about it. We probably overreacted a little bit. We started doing fewer rallies, which I regret now. So you were effective from that standpoint. We took the bait a little bit. The decision to go outside [for the acceptance speech] was one we didn't take lightly. We thought it was consistent with the kind of campaign we were going to run, with obvious weather challenges.

We had three big speeches. Obviously, there was Michelle Obama's speech, which ended up being very, very important. Her numbers changed, and stayed in the stratosphere for the duration of the campaign. That was important strategically; also, we were glad to see her image strengthen that way. [As for] the Biden speech and the Obama speech, we had to assume we [were] going to be able to get those right.

The big challenge for us was, obviously, all the drama around the Clintons and I think it came out about as well as it could have. The speeches by both the Clintons were great. The way that she came down to the floor, which was something we kept quiet and orchestrated, gave us a jolt of energy. We didn't expect there to be a lot of energy around the fact that Obama was nominated at the convention. That was a surprise to us. And for those of us on the floor and our field staff around the country it was a big deal.

So, we focused on those big moments and I think executed them pretty well. We had to grow the campaign, doubling and some case tripling our donors, volunteers, and e-mail list from June to November 4. We were able to do that. So we focused on, how do we get growth? So we did a lot of advertising. We did a lot of rallies, all in pursuit of trying to grow the campaign in the right places.

David Axelrod will talk a lot about message, so I'm not going to dwell on that. From a message standpoint, first, we wanted to be consistent. The consistency of our message: "change we can believe in" for 16 months in the primary, "change we need" for about four months in the general. Didn't deviate. It drove the press crazy. [They thought it] was boring [and] were annoyed by it. We think that constancy served us well, particularly for someone like the president elect, who was new to Washington.

Since there were questions about his experience, that solidity of message gave people over 22 months to get a sense that this guy had a core. He knew what he wanted to say. He didn't deviate much. We think we benefited from that more in the primary, where our opponent had seven or eight different slogans and different thrusts. We stepped back and said, "Maybe this constancy doesn't make survival in the 24 hour news cycle easy." But overall, it would wear very well.

Obviously, we needed to develop a crisper economic focus, both in contrast to Senator McCain, and in fleshing out our details. We probably got to that a little bit late in the primary. It caused us some difficulty in those last three months of the primary. So that was very important. But, the core message didn't change much. You need to change Washington. We need an economy that works for the middle class. If you look at our announcement speech in Springfield on February 10, 2007, many of its core elements were in the speech he gave November 3 [2008] in Manassas, Virginia, at eleven o'clock. It just didn't change very much. And that wore well.

We made a mistake in the primary at the very beginning when we didn't even have office space. We had to make a decision about federal money. We said, "Well, we will accept general funds," but we petitioned the FEC [Federal Election Commission] to see if people who did that had the ability to go [out of] in the system. They said yes. That's all we said and that we would want to negotiate with our opponent.

A junior researcher filled out a questionnaire from some campaign finance institute, and said, "Yes—period." That really boxed us in. That was not a position of the campaign, to be that declarative. So it caused us some difficulty, but I would say a few things about it. One is, we really did feel as if (and I know that our opponent probably questioned this, and some of the press did, [as did] the reformers) we had achieved some degree of public financing. We ended up with over three and a half million donors, [with an] average contribution under $90. Teachers, firefighters, nurses. We felt good about the way we were raising our money.

Second, the decision was not about the amount of money, it was about control. We wanted to control all aspects of our campaign. When David Axelrod and I did a lot of the independent expenditure advertising in 2004 for the DNC in the Kerry-Bush race, we had a devil of a time. We spent more money than the Kerry campaign did but had no sense, day to day, what they wanted us to do. So, you sit there looking for smoke signals. Should we be negative? Should we be positive? They've lowered [their buy in] this market, I guess that means we have to go in here. Tonally, what should we do? That experience was searing to us. So we wanted control of our advertising, and most important, we wanted control of our field operation. We did not want to outsource these millions of people, and these hundreds of thousands of full-time volunteers to the DNC [Democratic National Committee] or any other entity.

So everything we did, including three tracks of advertising, radio, internet advertising, the field, was coordinated. And Jon [Carson] and I spent a lot of time talking about this. We wanted those volunteers at the door on October 20 in Roanoke, Virginia, to be as crisp in what they were saying as our advertising and our [candidate] was. And the only way to have that done was maintaining control over everything. . . .

Coming out of the primary, we were now the nominee of the Democratic Party; it was very important for us not to lose that insurgent, outsider feel. So now, we had to work with all the interest groups and the elected officials. And one of the great benefits of the primary is, for the most part, we won without their help. I think it's one of the reasons [President-elect Obama's] got a chance to be a successful president is we don't owe a lot of people in Washington very much.

So one thing that was very important was not changing who we are. We're a grass roots campaign; we're going to make decisions in the interest of our candidacy; we are not going through the old dusty Democratic general election play book. That made some of our politics hard, but we were able, with some struggle, to maintain that. And it was very, very important. I think we would have been much less successful if we had become an institutional candidacy.

In our campaign, we always said, the most important word is no. We said no a lot in the general election, because we had to retain focus. [The McCain campaign] kept us on our toes every single day.

I remember, at the end of the campaign, people wanting money for Senate and House races and suggesting we travel to Minnesota to help the Senate candidate there. We don't have this thing put away, okay? The [McCain campaign is] out there every day, banging away. McCain's traveling around the clock. You can't rest and let up until you've won. And so, we were very focused on our own race, and thought that to the extent that we generated a good turnout that would help other candidates. That was our big contribution. But we weren't about doing anything other than getting 270 electoral votes.

Finally, the map. We were very transparent about this. I did a press conference in Washington in June, where we talked about our big map. [The press conference] was largely met with derision. "Indiana and North Carolina, Georgia, even Virginia and Florida, what are you guys thinking? It's all spin. You're just trying to bait the McCain campaign." Our decision had nothing to do with the McCain campaign spending money.

If, as it turned out in the end, they had to spend more time and money in Indiana and North Carolina than they would have liked, that

CHART 2. 2004 ELECTORATE RESULTS

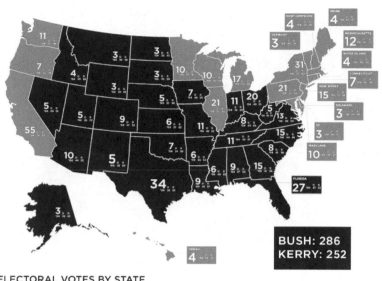

ELECTORAL VOTES BY STATE
ELECTION RESULTS '04 (%)

BUSH: 286
KERRY: 252

CHART 3. 2008 INITIAL TARGETS

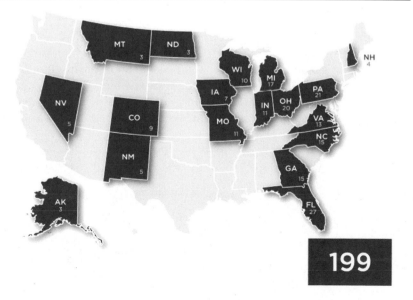

199

CHART 4. 2008 REVISED TARGETS

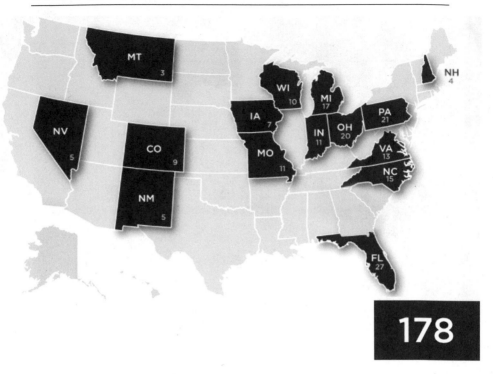

was a great benefit. But we went in there because we thought we could win. And this is where the primary was a big benefit. We had spent a lot of time in these states. In Indiana, we got 13 percent of the Republican vote. It was our highest Republican share in any battleground state. In North Carolina, we thought we could get the kind of turnout that we needed. Same thing in Virginia, where we thought we'd do very well with independent voters.

So these were very hard decisions. They required an enormous amount of money. Obviously, if we were in the federal system we would not have been in these states. Second, it required an organization. And particularly, when your candidate is Barack Hussein Obama, who's new to the scene, you need that kind of field organization, those people in their communities, talking with their neighbors and their colleagues about the election. We studied the Bush [2004] campaign pretty carefully. They did a great job.

I don't think any of the people we ran against in the primary could have done it. We were blessed to have this grass roots energy. This isn't all about a plan. People were motivated, not just to give us money and volunteer occasionally, [but] we had people who were giving us 20, 30, 40, 50 hours a week, who had one, two, three jobs. It was a remarkable thing. And it made us a great campaign. It helped us with turnout and persuasion.

So that map was critical. We were simply not going to wake up on November 4 waiting for one state to come in. We were going to try and put these states in play. Now, in the beginning, did I think we would win as many states as we did? No. We pulled out of Georgia and North Dakota and Alaska and went back into a couple of them in the last four days. The only two target states we lost of our core group were Missouri and Montana. So we had a high degree of success. Won some states like Indiana, North Carolina, pretty narrowly, Florida too. But it was very important for us to have a lot of different avenues. We did think it would put pressure on the McCain campaign financially, and from a candidate travel perspective. But we thought we had the organizational and financial ability to do that.

In September, I can't tell you how many people said, "You guys are out of your minds. You need to just retrench into Pennsylvania, Ohio, and Michigan, and give up this ridiculous quest for these other states." Right after [the Republican] convention, I did an interview in the *New York Times*, and purposely used the term bed-wetters to send a message to our party to calm down. Just calm down. We know what we're doing here. This strategy makes sense. We want to stretch the playing field.

We basically started out with 14 Bush states, only 4 Kerry states. And as time went on, that ratio maintained itself. We put enormous pressure on [the Republicans]. From an Electoral College perspective, they had a much tougher job than we did. We had a lot more avenues to get there. That map informed everything we did just as Iowa informed everything we did in the primary for 12 months.

The next slide is our initial target list, which we announced in June, which was the 18 states. The next is our revised target list. And that's really what we lived with until the last week of October, when we added back in Arizona, North Dakota, and Georgia.

We got over 45 percent of the vote in all three of those states. So, the truth is, if we'd had a little bit more time and money, we might have been able to pull one out, particularly Georgia. It was really hard to pull out of Georgia because it was clear [that] if we campaigned the whole time there and Obama went there, it was going to be a one or two point race, in our view.

Jon Carson

Jon Carson worked on the Obama campaign from February 2007 through November 2008: as Illinois state director through July 2007, as national voter contact director overseeing planning for the primary contests after the four early states, and as national field director for the general election. Carson was campaign manager for Tammy Duckworth's congressional campaign in 2006, and was a coordinated campaign director in New Jersey in 2003, South Carolina in 2002, and Iowa in 2000. He served two years in the Peace Corps as a water and sanitation engineer from 2004 to 2006 and has an M.A. in Geography from UCLA.

An interesting thing about our field organization is [that] probably 85 percent of the staff we had and 75 percent of the volunteers had never been involved in a campaign before. I had to remind them quite often that we didn't invent this stuff. The idea that a neighbor knocking on a voter's door was a good thing had been around for a while. The highly structured, accountable system we put in place for our volunteers wasn't new either. They'd been doing it in Chicago for a hundred years.

What was new was the scale on which we were able to do it and the accountability. There were three key elements to that. The first one is obvious. You can have all the thoughts in the world, but if we didn't have a motivational candidate, we wouldn't have had the raw numbers that we had. The second piece was misinterpreted by the press a lot. Our online efforts were a net, they weren't the engine. At the end of the day, voter contact happened because trained field organizers got their volunteers into a system that was getting doors knocked and phone calls made. What the online efforts allowed us to do was grab these people quickly.

When we were hopping from state to state in the primary, we were able to go into Texas with three and a half weeks to go, had a quarter of a million volunteers signed up, with phone numbers, e-mail addresses. They had been using our social networks to form themselves into teams. A behind the scenes piece to this, which I do have to credit to the DNC, was that, finally, the party had a national voter file.

And so, when we started this general election, we had a system in place. Despite this decentralized system, I knew every single morning how many phone calls had been made, how many doors had been knocked, where, by whom, and if there was anything funky in the data. With David's approval, we ran what I call a Wikipedia style approach to data. Typically the Democratic party is concerned about who's touching the data, who's doing the data entry. [Instead] we put it out there. We trained our volunteers. We trusted them.

Jon Carson

The third piece to this was our organizing philosophy. How we used these volunteers ended up being crucial. Usually, the local mayors, the local elected officials got to meet the candidate. [In our campaign] our best team leaders [did that].

I called our office strategy our Starbucks strategy. We wanted offices everywhere because, despite all the focus on the online network, the truth of the matter was where we had offices and volunteers were working together with staff, we got work done.

We didn't have the three months that the McCain campaign had. But one opportunity we had on the field side was when Indiana and North Carolina were over on May 6 . . . we brought in about two dozen of our best field people from around the country and sat them down for a month to figure out what had worked and what hadn't.

We learned how to use this massive group of volunteers that we had. One assumption we made from the beginning was that half the value of this wasn't in the doors they knocked or the phone calls they made as part of an organized structure, but [was] that on Sunday, after knocking doors on Saturday, they'd go to church and tell all their friends and neighbors they were part of the Obama campaign, and how excited they were. If you make phone calls from San Francisco, you might remember the next day to make sure your cousins in Ohio vote as well.

The most important part of that massive group of people were the super volunteers that we had. We figured out in the primary how to take advantage of them. What we really ended up having was an extra layer of staff out there. In Ohio, we had over 1,400 people who were putting in 20, 30, 40 hours a week, and we empowered them. In a difficult decision, and after a struggle with people who'd done campaigns before, we actually gave volunteers log-ins to our databases, access to all the other volunteers in their area, and told them to get the job done.

The mission we were given on the persuasion side was that our volunteers would really be validators. To win these Republican states, you have to persuade people who had never voted for a Democrat before. A lot of that is peer pressure, frankly. And so we put a top premium on local volunteers talking to their neighbors, and the mission that David gave us was having these volunteers be up to date with what was going on.

If we were putting out a new ad, our volunteers knocking doors that night should know what it was. That system was difficult to put in place, but I think we got there. At the end of the day, the most effective thing someone was able to say at the door was why they were supporting Barack Obama. [What mattered] was the fact that their neighbor was there saying, "this is okay, let's vote for this guy."

The Obama campaign took ownership of getting voters registered. And, I think, we significantly changed the electorate in a bunch of these states. Reporters would ask, "How did early vote change your strategy?" It didn't change our strategy. It was our strategy. We sat down and said "where early vote is no excuse, and convenient, we will begin the day that early votes start." [We engaged in] voter contact as though it was Election Day. We really learned how to use early vote in North Carolina during that primary. They have a fantastic system of one stop early voting there. You can register and vote at the same time.

The other lesson that we carried from the primaries into the general was a concept I called field information campaigns. Traditionally, Democrats rent some vans, drive around, throw people in the van, take them to the court house, and vote them. We knew that our supporters were energized. Maybe they hadn't voted before, perhaps they hadn't been registered but they wanted to participate.

We put a premium on just getting [needed] information out there [using] our massive internet advertising program and having field people focus on building a crowd in front of an early voting location in

North Carolina, to get it on the six o'clock news. Far more people were going to get information [from such a news segment] on how to do it, and show up and vote, than you ever could have driven there one at a time.

Our Get out the Vote (GOTV) efforts were the culmination of this empowerment strategy. We went after weak voting Democrats wherever they were. In southeast Ohio, we were knocking on doors in precincts that had never seen it before. Our organization allowed us to do that.

A lot of reporters asked about our targeting strategy, our data strategy. I believe that we had the best data that any Democratic campaign was able to use in a presidential. With such a broad organization in suburban Alexandria, [for example] in a Republican precinct, if someone moved in next door to one of our supporters, might be a 50-year-old white male, that person wouldn't show up on anyone's targeting list. [If the neighbor learned that the newcomer was supporting Obama, he'd say] "Let's get you registered. Let's get your data in." Our broad-based organization allowed us to move past some of the typical stereotypical targeting.

The toughest piece, and what differed from past Democratic campaigns, was that, from the moment those offices were ready, until the convention speech, the only thing I ever hounded them on was how big is your organization? How many people have you trained? How broad-based is it? Those were the numbers we were reporting on every single night. [The day after the convention speech—we launched the] the army that we needed for registration, voter contact, and then rolled seamlessly into GOTV.

The scale of voter contact that we achieved was pretty enormous. What allowed us to grow exponentially at the end was the base of super volunteers that we had. You can't, with just a couple hundred staff in a state, put on the kind of operation we had. Traditionally, Democrats have two or three hundred giant labor union parking lots full of canvassers the final weekend. We wanted 1,400 across a state like Ohio. Living rooms, garages, and backyards were going to be our staging areas. I think we got that done.

We have some data on what the field effort was able to do in terms of persuasion. We had two tracks going on. We were constantly identifying people through paid phones. We saw that repeated contact by their neighbors resulted in higher support for Senator Obama.

This was very gratifying. There were a lot of questions about early vote. We won't know what happened in the election until voter files are repopulated and we see who actually voted. Did we win because we turned out more people, or because we switched votes? We don't know

CHART 5. ACTIVE VOLUNTEERS AND WEEKLY CONTACTS

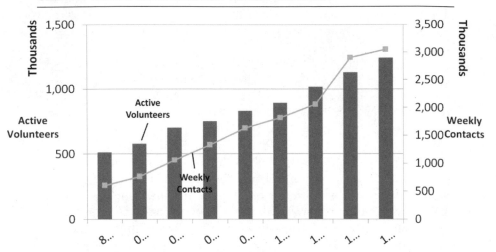

that yet, but we do see from early voting that if we talked to people, and they were sporadic voters, 8 percent more of them turned out and voted early. We had slightly more marginal affect on likely voters. If you're a fired up 64-year-old grandmother, and we told you how to vote early, you're going to make sure your sporadic voting kids and grand kids are doing it too. So that was the strategy.

We do believe we turned out a lot more of our sporadic voters and new voters to vote early than the Republicans did. And that held across all the states that had significant early voting. Here we have the final results.

We had the ground to ourselves. For months, we were able to build an enormous organization. Those field operations we had in Oregon, Washington, Maine, Minnesota, who had no air cover, had no support, were getting the job done, were getting those ballots in, those vote by mail states, so that all the resources could be pushing the envelope out in those other states.

DAVID PLOUFFE:

In most battleground states, we had three or four tracks of advertising. An underappreciated part of the campaign was the two-minute ads we did. We did the first one on the economy, and it really made an impact in these [key] states. It was not a traditional political advertisement—

Those two-minute ads were a big deal for us as was the 30-minute pro-

CHART 6. SPORADIC AND NEW REGISTRANT EARLY VOTERS BY PARTY

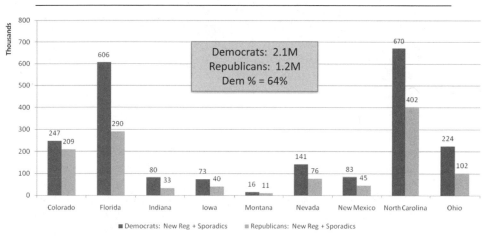

Democrats: 2.1M
Republicans: 1.2M
Dem % = 64%

■ Democrats: New Reg + Sporadics   ■ Republicans: New Reg + Sporadics

gram. One of my concerns was there're 20 days between the last debate and the election. Now, in the early vote states, that's less of an issue. In North Carolina, Nevada, not an issue. But in the other states, and I think that's probably one of the reasons you guys wanted Pennsylvania, there wasn't going to be much early voting there. So, if things broke late, there weren't a lot of votes in the bank for us.

We needed to do a couple of things in that period that weren't just barnstorming around. So we did the 30-minute ad, which, again, went well. It could have bombed. And we went through a lot of different discussions about how to do it. We also did a couple of economic summits as just things to try and have something out of the norm. In the beginning, we didn't know we'd, quote unquote, win all three presidential debates.

So even without that, we thought, that's going to be a long 20 days for us. For him [Senator Obama] to be talking directly to folks about what he wanted to do, and never saying anything about his opponent, was a huge benefit for us. And the McCain campaign just didn't have that ability.

JON CARSON:

On the field side of it, the money can come in from different directions. [Things would have been different if] we had run that through the DNC. I've run three coordinated campaigns. That kind of messaging turns into a three-humped camel that isn't doing anyone any good. I fundamentally believe that we did more for house candidates, and senate candidates, and gubernatorial candidates by just going out there, with early vote, and GOTV, but doing it in the Obama name. We brought in new voters, and didn't have to negotiate with people over what that [process] was going to look like.

DAVID PLOUFFE:

The period in June was tough because state parties, senate candidates, and gubernatorial candidates were saying, "What are you guys doing? Just send money to the party, and we'll take care of things." And we said, "No, we're not doing that. We're going do our own persuasion. It's going to be Obama persuasion. These people are going to be working for Obama, and we're going to do a lot of registration. And, you know, in a way, we gave them a lot of financial relief through all that. Most of them didn't think it was going to work to their benefit, but in the end it did. But those were tough internal discussions, because it hadn't been done that way before.

STEVE SCHMIDT:

How many staff did you finish up with?

DAVID PLOUFFE:

Well, a lot of them were 60 or 90 day, but we were over 5,000 at the end. We ended the primary at about 750 or 800.

STEVE SCHMIDT:

One of the things that I think speaks to the brilliance of your management of this campaign was your ability to manage the exponential, and, in my view, organic growth of the campaign, from the announcement in Springfield through that first quarter, where I think you raised $25 million, and then this just explodes.

You were able to put a fence around this rapidly growing, organically growing, exponentially growing thing. I wouldn't think you would have anticipated the chord that he struck in that time frame.

DAVID PLOUFFE:

Well, Steve, the scale of it certainly took us by surprise. I think the scale at the end of the campaign was a little bit less surprising than what we were able to do in 2007. First, we had a talented senior staff. We were fortunate that when we started this campaign, it was very untraditional. Most people plan to do this for a long time. They've got people pegged for positions. They've been to Iowa and New Hampshire. We had none of that.

And in many respects, it made those first months grueling as all get out. But I think we were a better campaign for it, because we were much more nimble. But we had a lot of great people who gravitated to the campaign. People in this room who were just great, and creative. And I think that we, from the beginning, knew that as a distinct underdog against Hillary Clinton we had to run a grass roots campaign. It's what Senator Obama wanted to do. We thought it was our only opportunity to win. And so, the value of these people infused the entire campaign. It was in our core. It's the only reason we won the primary.

In Iowa in 2008, if the electorate of 2004 had shown up, we would have lost the caucuses. In September, we said, "If we do not get this share of younger voters under 30–35 out we're just not going to win." There were as many people under 30 in the Iowa caucuses as over 65. We accomplished the Holy Grail. The only reason we were able to do that was the strength of our volunteer organization.

Low dollar events [were another opportunity]. We did the first low dollar fund-raising event in Kentucky. And, some people and I were skeptical about it, because we didn't think we would net money at all. It takes an enormous amount of staff to put it on. This is in the spring of '07. Lo and behold, 5,000 people come out. They're paying 25 bucks apiece, and the volunteers put it all on. Minimal staff. Remarkable thing.

You put 6,000 people in a room in Minneapolis, one staffer works on it. It was really the art of the possible. Our campaign became that. From a budget perspective, from a volunteer perspective, we had to think about what now is possible. What can we do to keep growing this thing?

We went into the February 5 states much earlier than we [anticipated] because the revenue was greater. We had the organizational pop that permitted us to send six staff into a caucus state, and do a lot of damage.

One of the big challenges in '07 was what do we have these people do? They all can't go to Iowa. So we had to help them grow the campaign. We'd say, "Find us ten more people to sign up on the e-mail list." That would frustrate them sometimes, and we'd say, "Just trust us. Just do that. It's going to end up being a big deal." When we got these February 5 states, that took a lot of the political pressure off because people had three or four months to work in their states.

PETER HART:

How much of this is transformational? In other words, it worked well for Barack Obama, but would it have worked for Chris Dodd, or for Joe

Biden, or anybody else? In other words, how much have you changed the system, or is it really only a change if you have a candidate as special as Barack Obama?

DAVID PLOUFFE:

I think it's the latter. If Hillary Clinton or John Edwards or any of these people had been nominated, it would have been a much different race from the map perspective, but also the organization. If he runs for reelection, it's not going to be the same election. I think you're going to see a lot of people try to replicate what we did. And I think that would be a mistake. But I hope belief in volunteers continues. It's a good thing.

I think that we did some smart things in the campaign, but it's all bells and whistles without the candidate. I think it's all candidate-based.

JON CARSON:

In the primaries, Bill Richardson had the exact same website technology we did. He used the same company. He just didn't have as many people on it.

MARK WALLACE:

Can you talk about your initial budgeting, what you planned? I'd like to hear what you actually thought you would raise?

DAVID PLOUFFE:

June, July, and August were right on target. September and October were probably a combined $50 or 60 million over. We actually thought we were going to raise a lot of money.

Now my view was [that] advertising was less important in the presidential election then in some other races, just because of the intense interest. People have a lot more information.

We were spending, I thought, enough on media to win the race if we had raised what we projected. But it would have been much more competitive.

We prioritized field operations because we believed we needed to adjust the electorate, we had to have human beings having conversations with human beings in places like Lorain, Ohio. We needed that 65-year-old white retired steel worker to say—"You know, maybe I'm surprised, but I'm for Obama, and here's why." That's something we learned in the primaries. We had to have those validators out there.

NICOLLE WALLACE:

I wonder how much of Bush '04 you used, and what you discarded, and, did anything go wrong? We felt as if something went wrong for us every fourth day. What were your crises, if there were any?

DAVID PLOUFFE:

We did study Bush 2004 pretty carefully. I thought that the Bush reelect campaign was a better campaign than 2000. What the Bush people did on turnout was remarkable. I didn't think a Republican could find that many unregistered Republicans.

One of the things that gave us confidence was that John McCain didn't just have to replicate the turnout in states like Ohio and Florida that Bush got, he needed to increase turnout by 10 or 12 percent. The Lieberman discussion is interesting because it might have changed the whole dynamic and your independent share gone up.

We studied [the Bush campaign] very carefully, especially the discipline of those campaigns. Obama actually said, in the very beginning, I like the Bush model of a few people in a room making decisions who don't talk to the press about it. We tried to instill that.

We made plenty of mistakes. You look back to the primary, and this is my mistake: if we had spent more time and money on Texas, as compared to Ohio, we probably would have won the Texas primary, and we might have been out of the primary. Big mistake. Huge mistake.

In New Hampshire we probably could have adjusted things differently. There were some things happening there outside of our control. But, we didn't handle those four or five days well at all. [The perception that we were engaged in] a triumphant march across New Hampshire cost us.

JIM MARGOLIS:

I think we were thrown off a bit right after the Palin announcement. There were a couple a days there where we were all looking at each other. . . . We just didn't have our footing there for a couple a days. I think we believed, at the end of the day, it was going to come back.

I was sent in to talk to our Hill friends. People said, "Okay, one, when are you going to go after her? When are you going to go after him? When are you going to go to Keating?" It was that kind of craziness. You'd just say, "Everybody's just going to have to take a deep breath here. Let's wait a couple of weeks, and let this settle down."

DAVID PLOUFFE:

That was a tough period for us. There's something very dynamic happening in the race, [but] I thought it was all going to settle down eventually. What goes up that high comes back down.

I think some of us thought the computer ad was a good idea.[1] I pushed for it. I think it was probably a mistake in retrospect. What was the point of it really? It was not a smart thing to do.

JON CARSON:

From the field perspective, I don't think the win we ultimately had would have been as big if we wouldn't have had those two weeks because we had our own Palin effect. We had people reinvigorated. We saw a bump in our volunteer numbers. A mistake I think we made from the field side, actually, occurred early in June when I was emphasizing online contact too much. I thought that was going to expand further than it ultimately did. We never really got past the point where the online portion [of the campaign] captured people, who were very quickly enfolded into a traditional model.

ANITA DUNN:

In the second week of September we should have gone back to rallies earlier.

DAVID PLOUFFE:

You guys did a good job on spooking us on the rallies.

ANITA DUNN:

You really did. We just should have been a little nimbler and just taken him back to rallies. [Moving to more use of] the prompter [for both Biden and Obama] was a large decision that we should have gotten to much earlier.

JOEL BENENSON:

To echo what Anita said, one of our mistakes was not reacting as soon as Sarah Palin had a crowd of five, seven, ten thousand people. We should have said, "Let's go back, and reassert momentum."

DAVID PLOUFFE:

It took us a few days.

ANITA DUNN:

Yes, it did.

JOEL BENENSON:

The press immediately latched on to the notion that you had momentum. We knew we had the capacity, at any moment, to produce that, and we waited a few days. I think Anita's right, we should have been a little more nimble on that front.

ANITA DUNN:

I think we were just so caught in the idea that we needed to be portraying something different coming out of [the convention acceptance speech at] Invesco [Field].

JON CARSON:

An enormous benefit we had [was the fact that] we walked into the general election with 500 staff who'd been through hell and back for 15 months. They started as organizers in the early states. . . .

They all turned into regional field directors. So we were walking in with this incredibly young, but incredibly experienced and talented group of people, who'd seen six election days.

They'd seen volunteers of different types in six or seven different states. When you talk about mistakes in field, it's not enormous strategic mistakes; it's a thousand of them every single day. Is the office messy when you walk in? Are volunteers taken care of when they come in? So a strength that we had was that many of our field organizers had been volunteers.

We put accountability on them from the very beginning. We had a centralized database. If your doors or phone contacts weren't in there, they didn't count for anything.

DAVID PLOUFFE:

One small thing that's interesting, given the number of people we were trying to register, people who were sporadic voting Democrats: in caucus states we won like Minnesota, Colorado, Nebraska, our initial research had us trailing Hillary Clinton. Among core caucus attendees, she would beat us. So we had to expand the electorate.

We spent a lot of money advertising caucus and primary look-up tools, where people would type in a caucus location. With technology, you know who these people are. So, in the caucus states, in the primary, we'd say, "You know, Steve Schmidt just looked at his location. He's undecided. That's a lead. Let's go talk to him." In the primary it was over a million people who looked up these primary caucus look-ups. A lot of our people were new to states. They didn't know where their voting location was. They hadn't early voted before. So we spent hundreds of thousands of dollars on advertising just to try and show people how to caucus, where to vote, how to early vote.

Jon Carson:

The best story on that was the Hawaii caucus. Wisconsin and Hawaii were the same day. CNN calls Wisconsin for Obama at about 8:30 central time. It's five hours until the caucuses start in Hawaii. We had the look-up tool. Wolf Blitzer mentioned that there's a caucus later in Hawaii. When you typed that into Google, our ad popped up. 6,000 people looked up their location from the time they [the networks] called Wisconsin until the start of the Hawaii caucus.

Only 18,000 showed up for that caucus in support of us. The look-up tool probably won us two convention delegates. So that's what I think is transformational. There have always been people who wanted to get involved. Now we can find out that they looked it up and call them back the same day.

Note

1. "Still" aired mid-September 2008:

Announcer: "1982. John McCain goes to Washington. Things have changed in the last 26 years. But, McCain hasn't. He admits he still doesn't know how to use a *computer*. Can't send an e-mail. Still doesn't understand the economy and favors 200 billion in new tax cuts for corporations, but almost nothing for the middle class. After one president who was out of touch, we just can't afford more of the same."
Barack Obama: I'm Barack Obama and I approve this message.
Graphic: Approved by Barack Obama. Paid for by Obama for America.

Chapter 3

Campaign Organization and Strategy

Steve Schmidt

Steve Schmidt *is a partner of Mercury Public Affairs. He most recently served as a senior advisor to Sen. John McCain's presidential campaign. He provides high-level counsel to political candidates, elected officials, and major corporations. In 2006, he served as campaign manager for the reelection of California governor Arnold Schwarzenegger. Schmidt is a former deputy assistant to the president and counselor to the vice president. He played a leading role in the confirmation of Chief Justice John Roberts to the Supreme Court and led the nomination team for Justice Samuel Alito. In 2004, he served as one of the top strategists on President Bush's reelection campaign.*

First I'd like to congratulate David and his entire team. It was a brilliant campaign. We look back with a lot of admiration for your accomplishment. Incredibly formidable. And unfortunate to be opposed to you.

Before I talk about some of our strategic assumptions, I want to lay out a fundamental difference between the McCain and Obama campaigns. In July 2007, John McCain's presidential effort was upside down and in a ditch. He was in last place in the polls. The campaign was dead broke. Most of the staff had been let go or resigned. His victory in the Republican primaries is, I believe, one of the greatest comebacks in the history of politics.

On the day that he secured the nomination, March 4, the campaign had a total staff at headquarters of 38 people and was dead broke. From a resource perspective, in the intervening months, we were in a race to come up to even a minimalist level staffing, [and even if we were able to do that we would not be able] to be competitive against the Obama campaign, which was blowing the doors off and setting record after record in all manner of areas. [We were in a race] just to be competitive from an organizational perspective against your typical presidential campaign, John Kerry's for example.

You can't run a campaign with 38 people. So the campaign had difficulty through the spring. Lots of growing pains. Lots of execution fail-

Steve Schmidt

ures from lighting to teleprompters, all evidence of a lack of money and staff. That issue was embedded in our operation all the way through.

The amount of money the Obama campaign raised is historic and staggering. It was amazing to watch and be on the other side of. With the weight of [their] television advertising and field program we felt as we moved into September and October that we were surrounded and being closed in on in a very dramatic sense. In states such as Indiana, we were outspent seven to one. The financial disparity was enormous. It was difficult to compete.

The other thing David said, which I think is a critical part of a successful campaign at this level, is [that it's important to have] the ability to have complete and total control over all of your messaging, to have control over your operations. Because of our decision to stay in public financing, we did not have [complete] control over those things. [Finally] in October, we made a decision to stop doing the hybrid ads and to ship all the remaining money to the RNC, to an independent expenditure that we had no control over and no contact with. We kept the remaining money to do our ads. [We made that decision] on the simple basis that the hybrid ads that the campaign was producing made no sense.

In a meeting, [in which we] talked about the hybrid ads, somebody used the line "[watching the hybrid ads] was like watching a Fellini film on acid." I was living in Virginia from July forward. On television at night you'd see the beautiful [Obama] 30 second ads and the two minute ads. The weight of advertising was just remarkable. And the ads were great. You'd [only] occasionally see a McCain ad.

We had very talented media consultants working for the campaign. Under the [constraints imposed by the] hybrid rules, I don't care how talented you are, it's very difficult to drive two messages, particularly when one of those is a generic one that has to be a Republican message. In the big structures at work in 2008, people were very angry at Republicans, and very open to Democrats across the board.

So, our strategic premise in this race really from the get go was that we were running a campaign in the worst environment ever and that environment was continuing to worsen. We were running a campaign in a very bad economy and the economy was continuing to worsen. We were running a campaign as the nominee of the incumbent party in the White House with record low approvals and his approval levels were continuing to worsen.

If you view a campaign as a race to the top of the mountain, no campaign ever starts out exactly even. One campaign is always going to have an advantage over the other and that advantage may manifest itself, to continue the analogy, in a 30-minute head start up or a four hour head start up the mountain. In our case, it felt as if the Obama campaign was walking up a side of the mountain on paths. Still a rigorous challenge [but on paths nonetheless]. On our side of the mountain, you needed ropes and ice axes and any slip led to certain death. . . .

So [starting with] a couple of guys with Senator McCain on a bus, we had to put together a real campaign. Whether we could have done it faster or better, I'm sure there were a lot of mistakes made at that time. But people and particularly the press never appreciated the state of the campaign that actually won the nomination, how broke it was and how few people were part of it.

So, we come forward to Senator Obama winning the nomination. We do an event in Louisiana. From a positioning perspective, we had tried to introduce the story of John McCain's life: John McCain's a different type of Republican. He'd done environmental events. We went through Selma, Alabama, and to impoverished places that had been forgotten in the country. These events were largely ignored by the national media. [They weren't considered] a particularly compelling story, when [on the other side] you had the most exciting political contest that anyone, including us, had ever seen. We watched with a lot of fascination also. It was an amazing race to watch.

Since we weren't getting much coverage, we made a decision to come out on that first historic night when Senator Obama secured his party's nomination. Senator McCain gave a contrast speech: 900 people are left outside the room; they can't get in. The backdrop is this terrible green color. It was a systems failure of epic proportion, a true debacle. Because of that event, we were structurally on defense for weeks in the month of June. It was one of the mistakes that the campaign made. We should have stayed down or it should have been a speech with no contrast, a congratulatory speech that said "Let's have a good effort." It took us weeks to recover from that single night. The media narrative was not good.

One of the issues that we dealt with all through the campaign was Iraq. It was the issue that, more than any other, damaged Senator McCain in the early part of the campaign in the Republican primary. It did as much as any other issue to injure him politically and to diminish the difference in his brand, his difference from the president. He then used his advocacy for the surge to get back into the race and he won. He meant it when he said he'd rather lose an election than lose a war, and people understood that.

Senator McCain was right about the surge strategy. Iraq moved off the front pages of the election over the course of the spring and summer as the surge strategy began to succeed. And Senator Obama, challenged by Senator McCain to go to Iraq after 900 days, did what we suspected he was going to do and went to Iraq. It was pretty clear in observing the Obama campaign that not only were they going to have a successful trip, but it was going to be a great trip. There weren't going to be any mistakes or errors.

I'm a lifelong New York Jets fan. And, as a New York Jets fan, you know they can be in the playoffs, they can be up 14 points with two minutes left, and, I know how the game is going to end. It's not going to be a happy thing for the Jets fan. When it came to the Obama campaign, you knew what they were going to do extraordinarily well.

As he was moving through the world capitals, Senator Obama looked as if he should be standing on the world stage. He looked like a President of the United States. Everything about him, from how articulate he is, to the eloquence and gracefulness of his physical movements: he looked tremendous.

We were very worried at this point in the race that they were about to run away with this and it would be over. I've always believed in my career that if you can put the other guy down in the summer months, it's very hard for him to get back up. I had had an experience in 2006 [Schwarzenegger campaign] where we had done this effectively. You're informed by your previous experiences and we were very worried about that. Bill [McInturff] was at a small group meeting at the tail end of this trip. It was very sobering. The Gallup average, which we were watching pretty consistently, was opening 8, 9 points.

I had read something that talked about Barack Obama as a driver of merchandise. His face was now more popular than Bob Marley and Che Guevara on the tie-dyed tee-shirts. He was a product line. I said the next cycle I'm doing the merchandise side of this. I'm on the wrong side of this. So we came up with the concept that he's certainly a very talented political candidate, a once-in-a-generation candidate.

[We knew why] John Kennedy or Ronald Reagan stood in Berlin, why those people were coming out to see them. There's hopefulness, a new America. But [the reason people are attending is] it's also part of a celebrity culture. We used the "celebrity" ads as a tactic to try to stay in the race and to say something about Senator Obama that would resonate with people and raise a doubt about the excesses of enthusiasm from our perspective [which we humorously conveyed as] "The One."

Humor's an effective weapon in a campaign. In the month of August, beginning with a series of web videos, we were able to take some control of the viral space on YouTube, an arena [in which] we'd been just completely manhandled by the Obama campaign. In August, we began to have some success in competing virally.

We hoped over the course of the month to put a filter on the Invesco speech so that there would at least be a [media] debate about whether [the Obama acceptance speech at Invesco] was a smart or not a smart thing to do. [If we didn't create this alternative we anticipated] a month of discussion in the press about this most incredible moment in American politics. It worked. We evened the race. We then came to the Democratic Convention.

[Incidentally] one of the factors in this race was [that] the Republican Party is a smaller party than it was four years before and the Democratic Party a bigger one. [Moreover] although we had suggested that women and other constituencies that supported Senator Clinton weren't going to vote for Senator Obama, at the end of the day, we all believed that these Democratic constituencies would return home. We also knew that the Obama convention speech was going to be superb. We knew that President Clinton and Senator Clinton's speeches were going to be excellent, as well. We anticipated it being a very successful event.

We also knew that we had gone from eight or nine points back at the beginning of August to even at the end of the European trip. We even got ahead for a day or two in the Gallup tracks. After the Democratic convention, we were down 8, 9, 10 points. So we needed a very significant bounce from our convention.

[Consider] the constellation of available Republican candidates for Vice President and the political reality we were in. Sarah Palin was the most popular governor in the country. She had taken on her own party. She was a reformer. She had expertise on energy issues.

We began the summer's economic crisis [with a focus on] the housing stuff which was difficult for us because it's difficult for the conservative party's candidate to offer prescriptions. What the energy issue allowed us to do was to be active on an economic issue, by calling for an action the Democrats opposed.

It's more difficult if you're the Republican candidate in a housing crisis to say, "Here's what we prescribed that's interventionist from a government perspective." Four dollar [a gallon] gasoline gave us an opportunity to be active, to be interventionist on an economic issue. We took advantage of that and [energy was an] issue that had resonance and gave us currency through the summer. That issue was very much alive as we made the vice presidential selection.

Coming out of the convention, we had distanced ourselves from the unpopular administration, restored McCain's maverick appeal, made significant incursions into the middle of the electorate and excited the base.

We had always assumed that we needed to have some luck. We needed to throw the ball down the field. In the natural order of things, we were not going to win because of the environment.

At a dinner party in Los Angeles in the spring of '08, somebody told me they had attended one of David's [Plouffe] presentations on the campaign. They reported that David said that he wanted to make sure that on Election Day Senator Obama had a wide path to victory. I said, "Well, it's going to be a narrow path for us." There was never an option for our campaign to wake up with nine or ten different ways [to victory]. The environment didn't lend itself [to that] in a realistic way to that.

We got our post-convention bounce. We underwent a rescission, which we expected, and the race is essentially even. I don't think a lot of people expected us to be in an even race, given the environment in the middle of September.

Then the global economic catastrophe begins and goes through a two-week period. The event begins on that Monday with the collapse of Lehman Brothers [September 15]. Senator McCain was trying to talk about the workers, the foundations of the American economy [when he said "the fundamentals of our economy are strong"].[1] He's very hard on himself on this, harder than anyone else. He made an in artful turn of phrase and the Obama campaign was very good at capitalizing on mistakes. We were running a campaign against a team that was very punishing, very unforgiving. When we made a mistake, they were all over it.

So, we began this period of economic uncertainty on "the fundamentals of our economy are strong." We then had a campaign surrogate [Carly Fiorina] who said that he didn't have the ability to be CEO of a company.[2] I think we moved into the middle of this week on the economy very much back on our heels.

At the end of this first week of the economic [crisis] there is the notion that not only has there been a bad economic event but the entire global financial order will collapse unless there is $700 billion passed immediately and given to the treasury secretary to dispose of however he sees fit.

Now, I feel comfortable having a discussion on national security issues. I feel comfortable having a discussion on the difference between supply side and Keynesian economics. And I feel comfortable on energy policy and comfortable enough on health care policy to be somewhat dangerous in a discussion. However, I can't speak at any level on what a credit default swap is or isn't. . . .

The debate in the country was "We have to have the $700 billion, and why?" If you recall that weekend, Secretary [Henry] Paulson [Secretary of the Treasury, 2006–2009], and—Mr. [Ben] Bernanke [chairman of the Federal Reserve, 2006–current] go on the Sunday shows and tell Congress, "We must have this money."

The testimony [before Congress] and the appearances do not go particularly well. They do not do a particularly effective job [answering the question] "Why is this money necessary?"

As a policy matter, Senator McCain was opposed to giving a three-page, $700 billion blank check to Secretary Paulson, with no oversight or accountability as, I suspect, was Senator Obama. Both campaigns issued a set of principles, because I think both men understood that they had every potential to come out and tank the global economy. . . .

During this period, we are seeing unhappy poll numbers. We are no longer ahead. People are blaming the Republicans and the administration for this.

Senator McCain convenes his top economic advisors—John Thain, Stephen Schwarzman, Meg Whitman, Mitt Romney, people who do understand this. One thing was clear. Every person, Democrat or Republican, who knew anything about the economy, Larry Summers, Hank Paulson, and Warren Buffett, nobody that I'm aware of was saying that this $700 billion was unnecessary.

In fact what they were saying was that if this package was not passed by Monday, not by Tuesday, not by Wednesday, not by a week, but by

Monday, the global financial order would collapse in a devastating and catastrophic way.

At the beginning of that week, Senator [Majority Leader Harry] Reid said, "Well, the passage of this is really entirely in the hands of John McCain." House Republicans were saying, "Well, the passage of this is going to be up to John McCain." The White House was saying the Republican votes are going to be a function of John McCain.[3]

So, we were checkmated. The choices were: do you return to Washington to try to affect the outcome or stay outside Washington and hope for the best? If you stay outside of Washington, and the economy collapses, and everybody is already saying in the middle of the week that this is in your hands, you'll get the blame for it, particularly when you're running on the slogan of "Country First" and when you're trying to distinguish yourself from President Bush, who was criticized for his handling of Katrina because he wasn't on the ground. We thought it was a terrible choice but one made from a checkmated position. If the bill didn't pass, and the global economy collapsed, it would be over. And despite the representations of various members and Secretary Paulson that a deal to vote for this was in place, there was no deal in place and there were no votes for it.

As a United States Senator, Senator McCain wanted to go back to Washington to work on this, suspend his campaign, reach out, try to put a patina of nonpartisanship over it. When he went to the White House, a partisan spectacle broke out. The Democratic Party, and this is one of the things that you saw throughout the campaign, but really acutely at this moment, was hungry for victory. All hands on deck. Everyone on message. All hands kicking the crap out of John McCain, who is standing behind the podium all by himself, unsupported.

There was not a Republican effort to match the Democrats. The Republicans weren't there saying, this is a guy who's putting his country first as he did [in this instance and that]. He was unsupported and this issue was defined in a way that was not favorable to us.

On September 29, the Monday of the vote, I was on a plane with Governor Palin and watching the split screen of the markets collapsing and the bill being voted down. Then the news conference when the Republicans said they did this because Nancy Pelosi gave a mean speech.[4] I very rarely sleep on planes. But I took off my headphones (it was a Jet Blue charter) and fell asleep almost instantly like I was being anaesthetized in a doctor's office. I woke up several hours later. . . . .

In a general election for president, there are a number of days that are unequal to other days in the campaign: the three debate days, the nominating speech, and the vice presidential selection. I thought Senator McCain did a fine job in the debates. [However] our position was not helped by any of the debates. As a result, we were on a trajectory coming in to the final stretch of the race, where we were behind and the economy was falling apart. And in the third debate, the Obama campaign did a masterful job of stealing the tax issue from Republicans.

It was clear that in terms of who's going to give you a tax cut, who supports a tax cut for the middle class, [the answer in the debate] was Senator Obama is. If you're a Republican and you work on Republican campaigns, this is just the worst thing that could possibly happen, [particularly] when you look at his [Senator Obama's] record of voting for tax increases or against tax cuts.

The encounter with Joe the Plumber before the third debate defined the tax issue in a moment, in a way that we had been unable to define it for the entire campaign.

We were able to get some traction on fiscal issues, on tax issues, during the final stretch of the campaign and we saw some narrowing in the campaign. [We found some space within which to] differentiate ourselves from the unpopular administration and established that reform and maverick credential—once again. And we were viewed as a credible change agent.

The economic collapse blew up our strategy in the middle of September. We never went back to national security as an issue in the campaign, an issue [on which] we were strong. We were overtaken by a significant historic event, an unprecedented situation.

So, we were in a race in which we had no margin for error where we needed a little bit of luck. We didn't get the luck we needed, in order to do what we had to do to win the race. After the economic collapse, the right track numbers dropped to five percent. I don't believe that that's a number we'll ever see again, in any of our lifetimes. I certainly hope not.

It was very challenging to run a campaign in that environment, [especially] when you're running against a once-in-a-generation political talent running a campaign that was as close to flawless as a political campaign [can be].

DAVID PLOUFFE:

Did you have serious conversations about opposing the bailout?

STEVE SCHMIDT:

Never did. Not a single time. Because there wasn't anybody who was able to articulate a rationale for opposing it that didn't destroy the global economy. No one was going to say to John McCain, and I believe this is true of Senator Obama as well, "Well, we believe that this may have the effect of destroying the global economy, but we'll get a couple points out of it." That's not who John McCain is. There was never a discussion of it.

BILL MCINTURFF:

I was hired by John McCain in 1991 as part of the team to respond to Keating [the so-called "Keating Five" savings and loan scandal] getting ready for his '92 Senate Campaign. I've worked with him a very, very long time. If John were simply a U.S. Senator [and not the nominee of his party], I think he would have been the first person to oppose the bailout under its structure. As a U.S. Senator he would have been incredibly effective across the aisles putting together a [better] deal. . . .

And I would just say sardonically, after the failed vote, another eight days of that baloney, and then the market drops 1200 points. I think we said, "If someone had told us it's going to drop 1200 points anyway, we should been against it." Instead we were being told that to avoid that damage, you needed to vote for this. John's never said this, but I believe if he were in the Senate, and not running for President, he would have forcefully said, 'you can't give $700 billion on three pages of paper.' He would have forcefully been against it. He would have [brokered] a better deal and done it across the Senate. But you can't risk that as a candidate for U.S. President.

DAVID AXELROD:

Senator Obama called Senator McCain the morning that you guys announced that you were going to suspend your campaign. He called back some hours later and they discussed it. And he [Senator McCain] raised this notion of suspending the campaign. I think Senator Obama said, "Why don't we put a joint statement out and see what happens?" Did you know in those hours that he didn't call why Obama was calling?

STEVE SCHMIDT:

He was in debate prep, and in the McCain campaign we set new standards for procrastination when it came to debate prep. So, short of a massive attack on the debate prep location, we were not going to interrupt the debate prep. . . .

One of the things that I thought was a tremendous disservice to Senator McCain was the press's coverage of [the suspension of the campaign and return to Washington]. This was a person who had risked his political campaign on Iraq. Whether you agree or disagree with it, there's no question that he put it all on the line for an issue he believed in. This is a candidate who in the Republican primary [was told by us] 'the immigration thing is great. But maybe tone it down a little bit.' His response was "Not only am I not going to tone it down, I'm going to write the bill." So the notion that he didn't get the benefit of the doubt about trying to do the right thing there [in responding to the crisis by suspending his campaign], by the press, was unfortunate. The press narrative worked very well for you.

The notion repeated over and over in the press that John McCain blew up a deal that had existed was incredible to watch since there was no deal. We'd talk to reporters and say, "Why are you saying on your network that he blew up a deal, when you know there's no deal? You understand there's no deal." "We understand that." But, it was reported and that didn't work to our advantage.

JIM MARGOLIS:

Talk about what the relationship was going to be like with Bush. How you were going to handle Bush.

STEVE SCHMIDT:

For a number of us who worked for [President Bush] and were involved in the campaign, the fact that he had achieved record levels of unpopularity wasn't a happy thing, not a happy thing for any of us who's worked in Republican politics or in the White House. Everyone had personal affection for the president. Everyone wanted to be respectful to the office of president.

There are scores and scores of issues where John McCain and the president have differed over the years. We felt it was totally appropriate to talk about those differences and to talk about a different path. At the end of the day, though, all elections are about the future. And the future under a McCain presidency would have been different from under a Bush presidency. But [we weren't able to overcome] the weight of the wrong track number in the country, the weight of the President's unpopularity, the unpopularity of the party in some quarters.

One of the great ironies of this whole race is [evident when] you look at the Southwestern states, New Mexico, Colorado, Nevada, where I think that the Republican Party is deservedly punished by Hispanic and Latino voters. But the one guy who doesn't deserve to be punished by Latino voters and Hispanic voters was John McCain. Yet he was. I remember saying to the Hispanic ad team, "You job is [equivalent to that of] the first people who had to advertise for Tylenol after [seven people died from the Tylenol that had been tampered with] in the '80s." It was a tough road. So, on a number of those different issues, we just could not escape the general gravity of the climate.

ANITA DUNN:

Steve, Senator Obama entered the public financing system for the primaries and then took himself out once it became clear he could raise the money. We gave you a get-out-of-jail-free card on this issue when we went ahead and pulled out [of public financing] in June. I'm curious about whether you spent any time thinking about doing the same thing, given the fact that I think it's well known that John Kerry thought that was the single biggest mistake he'd made in 2004.

STEVE SCHMIDT:

Well, we didn't spend a great deal of time discussing it. Maybe we should have. But the fundraising operation was one area [in which] the campaign had struggled. We knew you would have more, but we believed we would have sufficient funds under public financing. And we did not believe, ultimately, that you would be able to raise the staggering amount that you were able to raise. I still don't have my arms around the amount of money raised.

[To be successful] the next Republican nominee [will have to run] really close to a billion-dollar campaign. Public financing is over.

ANITA DUNN:

When she announced her candidacy in January 2007, Hillary Clinton took herself out of the system. So, [the Obama campaign's decision] could not have been a surprise to anybody in the Republican Party.

DAVID AXELROD:

Could you have raised the money? If you had gone out of the system, what was your capacity to raise the money?

ANITA DUNN:

I think Palin would have let you raise a huge amount.

STEVE SCHMIDT:

I think we could have been more competitive financially if we had stayed out, but we would not have raised an equivalent amount [to what you raised].

DAVID PLOUFFE:

Of all the ads, the one that tested the best was the original maverick ad. Obviously, to Jim's question earlier, you jettisoned experience to pick Governor Palin. You put all your chips on reform. Absent the economic crisis, was that going to be the rest of September and October?

STEVE SCHMIDT:

Yeah. It had been reform/maverick. We were in a campaign where we were at five dollar gasoline. Part of the brilliance of your campaign was understanding the zeitgeist of the electorate, if you will, which was, people want a change and don't want Bush. You never deviated from it and you never had to. It seemed so obvious, in retrospect. If you're the Clinton campaign, it must make you wake up and scream at night.

David Axelrod

David Axelrod is one of the preeminent political media consultants in the United States, having produced winning media and messages for over 150 campaigns at the local, state and national levels. Most recently, Axelrod served as media advisor to President Barack Obama's campaign for the White House. In 2006, Axelrod oversaw the Democratic Congressional Campaign Committee's independent expenditure media program, helping Democrats regain the House majority for the first time since 1994. He has worked for leading Democrats across the country, including Senator Hillary Clinton in New York, Governor Tom Vilsack in Iowa, and Representative Rahm Emanuel in Illinois. A specialist in urban politics, Axelrod has produced victories for mayoral candidates in Chicago, Houston, Philadelphia, Cleveland, Detroit, and Washington, D.C.

We go at it hammer and tong during the campaigns, but I think we all have a lot of respect for each other. We know what it entails to be involved in these campaigns. And we know that we're all motivated by the same impulse to try and do something good within the system for the country.

This does remind me a little, for those of you who are old enough to remember, of the old Dick Van Dyke episode where Rob and Laura have a fight. They tell the same story only [for each] it's completely different. But the truth is [that] there's a lot of overlap [between your story and ours] that's really interesting.

Let's start here. In November 2006, when we were contemplating this race, I sent Senator Obama a memo. The first line said, "The most influential politician in 2008 won't be on the ballot. His name is George W. Bush. With few exceptions, the history of presidential politics shows that public opinion and attitudes about who should next occupy the oval office are largely shaped by the perceptions of the retiring incumbent. And rarely do voters look for a replica. Instead they generally choose a remedy, selecting a candidate who will address the deficiencies of the outgoing President."

We felt strongly that Obama's opportunity was that he represented the sharpest departure from George W. Bush, and the perceptions of George W. Bush. He [Senator Obama] was a healing and uniting figure at a time when people felt the country was too polarized. He was someone who was not particularly partisan at a time when people felt that there was too much partisanship in Washington. He was someone who had a history of advocacy for people and a big interest in fighting special interest influence at a time when the special interests were something that the public perceived as a major impediment to progress in Washington.

We felt as we looked at the field that no one running represented a sharper break from Bush. It was very clear when you looked at the drift of things. And it certainly turned out that way. This was going to be an election about change. The people wanted a profound change. In fact, through the two years of the campaign, each time we polled, and there are a number of pollsters in the room who probably had the same experience, and we posited the choice between a candidate who had years of Washington experience and a candidate who would bring fundamental change to Washington, the change candidate won.

This was true in the primary. It was true in the general election. Senator Clinton is an extraordinarily bright, incredibly tenacious person, and a very, very tough opponent. But inexplicably, for much of her campaign, until the end, her campaign presented her as the consummate Washington insider and ran her as an experience candidate, in an election that was plainly not about experience. That's what gave us the opportunity to win in what was really an uphill fight.

I heard Steve's comment about where his campaign was in the summer of 2007. We were 30 points behind in the national polls. Everybody in Washington was very generous with their advice about what we were doing wrong. But because it was a change election, we were able to win the nomination. So we come to a general election.

I can tell you that Senator Obama viewed Senator McCain as the most formidable potential opponent because of some of the attributes that Steve mentioned. In that same memo, I wrote, "John McCain remains the odds on favorite to win the Republican nomination. [He] is the best

David Axelrod

chance the Republicans have to break from Bush and offer their own version of change. His speech after the 2006 election to a conservative audience rebuking the party for 'drifting from its principles and reformist commitments' was excellent.

"McCain has a well-established reputation—as a feisty independent reformer." I'm skipping here. "Through his battles on such issues as campaign financing, remarks on environment, and his willingness to buck the President and his party on a wide range of issues. The GOP hierarchy, which almost always gets its man, seems resigned to McCain. But his nomination won't come without a fight or a cost. He remains anathema to many activists within the party from the religious right, which is deeply suspicious of his secular politics, to the tax cut purist, to K Street. He knows he will have a fight, and this has caused him to make a series of Faustian bargains with the right. From the dalliance with Jerry Falwell to his embrace of the anti-immigration panderers and gay marriage militants in his last campaign, McCain's straight talk express has taken many awkward detours.

"It'll be interesting to see how the Senator, who prides himself on his image of courageous principle, reacts when he's challenged on this down the line."

So, we had this notion that for John McCain to become the nominee of the party, he would have to make a series of Faustian bargains. Throughout the primary campaign, he was forced at times to defend his fealty to George Bush. As you know, there was a lot of tape of him talking about how he voted with Bush 90 percent of the time and [saying] he couldn't think of a major issue on which he had a disagreement with Bush, and so on.

We made good use of that tape throughout the campaign. It was very, very damaging because the one thing that was clear when the election campaign started was that as much as people in Washington and elites had a clear sense of who John McCain was, there wasn't a real clear sense among voters of who he was. Part of the benefit of a long and a well-publicized campaign is we were in the forefront although I must say, I realize now, you're absolutely right that we had some advantage, because we had the platform while you guys were [already] the nominee and sitting on the sidelines.

You know the old story about Winston Churchill. When he lost for prime minister in 1945, someone said, "Well, it's a blessing in disguise." And he replied, "Well, it's rather well disguised." When we were getting our brains beaten in by Hillary and her campaign, it didn't feel like a great benefit to us. But I can see your point.

But by the time we got to general election, people didn't know McCain that well. And one thing that was clear in all the focus groups that we did was that there was a fundamental concern that he would represent more of the same, that he was not enough change, that he was a little too much like Bush.

Our strategy from the beginning was to make this a race between "more of the same" and "real change." We drove that relentlessly through every speech, every platform. Now, having said that, when you win, people are filled with superlatives. And you hear "flawless campaign." The truth is that it took us a while to get organized. And there were a few things that you did that put us back on our heels.

We mishandled the drilling issue, without question. Any time you could do something to make yourselves the candidates of change against the status quo politics of Washington you were helping your candidate. In that one, we walked into a trap. We had many discussions about this in the aftermath of it.

[Senator Obama] was not dogmatic on the issue of drilling. He didn't have strong feelings about it other than [thinking] that it wasn't going to be the answer to [the country's] long-term energy problem.

You walked us into a trap. We walked into it. You were willing to do the courageous thing and break with the status quo on this issue and we were not. We stood with the Washington interest group on this issue. It took us some time to work through that issue. We shifted the discussion a little bit to the long term versus the short term and we made some headway, but we lost 17 points. We had a 17-point lead on energy when you started the drilling initiative. That [lead on energy] went down to zero. We lost some standing in the polls overall as a result.

Because we needed to show that Barack Obama could play on the world stage, that he was ready to be president and commander in chief, we had been talking for the better part of year about having to make a trip. We wanted to get that done. We wanted the whole fall to be about the economy. You're right that a global economic collapse helps in that regard, but we didn't know that was coming. We wanted to get this issue [ready to be president and commander in chief] out of the way so that we could focus on the economy.

We scheduled this trip about as late as we thought we could, in the last week of July. And you're right, the trip went very well. He performed very well on the trip. [Still] it was a high wire act and there were many places where the thing could have gone awry. Tiptoeing through Israeli politics or any number of other places, where something could have gone wrong. But it went well.

We did the speech in Germany because one of the things that people kept telling us over the course of two years was that they wanted to see a restoration of America's image in the world. We wanted to demonstrate that an American leader could speak about American ideals and still inspire an international audience to react in a way that was positive toward the country.

Interestingly, there was a lot of speculation at the time, and you probably fanned it, that we were going to speak at the Brandenburg Gate, where Kennedy and Reagan spoke.[5] When Senator Obama heard that that was one of the sites that we were actually scouting, he was incredulous. He said, "I'm not speaking there. I'm not President of the United States. It would be presumptuous to speak there." So, they moved it to the other end of the park, to the victory column there.

The day we got to Germany, he said, "I hope there'll be some people there." He was nervous that we weren't going to get a crowd.

I remember talking with Senator Obama about the fact that I thought there'd be some recoil on the trip. That it was so grand that there could be some pushback on it. At every point in the campaign when it looked like we were getting too big for our britches, people threw us back. I think there was a sense that Barack Obama had enormous potential but people weren't sure whether he had earned this opportunity. They wanted him to prove it. They wanted him to earn it. They were going to make us jump through every hoop and over every hurdle. And I think that's reasonable. I think they wanted to know that this guy was ready to be president of the United States.

When we won the Iowa caucuses and went to New Hampshire, it looked like we were doing victory laps. [By contrast] Senator Clinton was scuffling at ground level with people. It looked like she was fighting for it. And she won. As he [Senator Obama] said, "At the time, we were like Icarus flying too close to the sun."

Also the economy was getting worse. We were over there in Europe while people were struggling with the economy here. So, we felt there was some recoil.

You jumped into the void with your celebrity ads. We never really saw a tremendous backsliding as a result of those ads. They were not all that well received in our focus groups. But they dominated media coverage. You also sort of got into our heads. We also lost some space when Senator Obama took a vacation in the second week of August, his last chance to get away before the final stretch. While we were out of the picture, you made some real progress.

We knew we had to blast this thing back onto our turf. We wanted a debate about economic values. Republicans are always good about creating values debates. We felt that the way to overcome that was to turn the economy into a values debate. People were working hard and not getting what they deserved. . . .

We figured if you were going to come after us, it was going to be on taxes. So, we wanted to inoculate against that early. We had a middle-class tax cut from a year earlier. We pushed that issue hard. We also pushed the issue of lobbying reform because we thought that would short circuit your reform message and create a contrast that worked for us.

We pushed a contrast on health care. You had your program; we had ours. We could see how that could spin against us. People had mixed feelings about government intervention in the health care markets but they also wanted pre-existing conditions covered. They wanted regulation of some sort and they didn't want to pay taxes on their health care. We saw an opportunity there. And pushed every chance we could to line you up either with Bush or [with] policies that were Bush-like on the economy.

You say we weren't very forgiving about mistakes. We were forgiving. We just didn't want people to forget. We reminded them. In politics, small things become big if they're symbolic of something larger. Senator McCain appeared to have trouble recalling how many homes he owned. To people that was a symbol of someone who is out of touch. When you put it together with his support of $200 billion more in corporate tax cuts and with the Iraq war, which had become an economic issue, $12 billion a month for Iraq, nothing here, there was a growing sense that he was out of touch, a sense that he just didn't understand the economic experience people were having and the values argument began to grow.

We had a very clear plan for the convention speech. There are a few set pieces in campaigns that you have to get right. Then there are things that you can't plan on that you have to handle within the context of your message. The convention was something we had always counted on as a place to fill in the Obama biography, to make people more comfortable with him, and to drive our economic message.

On the Saturday before the convention, Joe Biden was announced as the vice presidential nominee. That turned out to be a great pick for us. Barack Obama was more than enough change for people. They wanted to see him surround himself with folks with a few gray hairs and a long resume. They wanted to know that there would be people around him to help him implement that change. Biden really fulfilled that.

He also was someone from Scranton, Pennsylvania who had a great profile with middle class voters and spoke to them in a compelling way. We gained some ground after Biden's appointment, which was on Saturday [August 23, 2008].

The first day of the convention was devoted to biography. Michelle Obama capped it off. She had a spectacular speech and increased her favorables by 12 points in one night and never looked back after that. The second night we drove the economic message and the economic contrast. Change versus more of the same message. Hillary Clinton anchored that for us and she was great.

The next night we had Bill Clinton, and Joe Biden. The focus was national security, giving people reassurance on that. Then came the speech at the stadium. Just to let you know how much you got into our heads, we were really sort of freaked out about it. We had committed to this. Plouffe and I cooked up this scheme to do it outdoors. Obama was completely skeptical. He said, "What if it rains? You guys are going to be standing there with umbrellas over my head if it rains."

After looking at all kinds of venues, we ended up in the stadium. One of the impacts of your "celebrity" campaign was that we started tearing down our big events. We were worried that we were looking too grandiose. [The fact that we anticipated] 80,000 people in a stadium was really a source of concern. Poor [Jim] Margolis had to go over there the night before the speech to rip out lights and all kinds of embellishments. We were trying to downscale everything at the final minute but we couldn't get rid of the columns. Everything else we ripped out.

You said that you thought that Obama would give a great speech. The fact is [that] we were on a rolling speechwriting mission right up to the end. The thing about him is that he writes when he writes. We actually had finished copy at 5:00 p.m. on the night that he gave the speech.

We had two run-throughs of the speech. The first was interrupted. There were three of us in the room with a prompter. He's five minutes into the first run of the speech when there's a knock on the door. Barack goes over to the door, opens it up and a guy says, "Did someone order a—a chicken Caesar?" It was my salad. He said, "Axelrod, I finally get to read the speech, and you're ordering a chicken Caesar right in the middle of my speech?"

But it was a superb speech. It reflected very much what we wanted to do, which was to go very hard at Senator McCain in an appropriate way. We wanted to look tough and firm and draw the distinctions while also leaving people with a sense of hope about the future.

He accomplished a lot in that speech. And as you said, we left the convention very happy. We then got on the plane and our Blackberries were going nuts. Sarah Palin's going to be the vice presidential nominee. Senator Obama said, "Hmm, that's really interesting. Why do you think he's done that?" And Senator Biden came over and said, "Well, what's goin' on?" I said, "Well, he chose Sarah Palin?" He said, "Who's Sarah Palin? And he said, "Governor of Alaska. Oh, yeah, I know her."

Our friends in Washington were in a complete lather about this because, if nothing else, it stirred the pot. There was this sense [among them] that we were gaining and you had stopped our momentum. And after she gave her speech, there was this sense that you had stolen the change mantle and he was going to ride this to victory.

Our attitude about it, at the time, was that you had blown up your message. You had spent the summer talking about celebrity and experience, and putting country first. Then you chose someone who wasn't experienced, made her a celebrity, and appeared to put politics ahead of the country in choosing an inexperienced candidate. And in one fell swoop you're competing with us on the realm of change, which is really our turf. So we weren't panicked about the choice.

The other thing, and this is why I asked this question before, Nicolle, is, it's very difficult to be parachuted into a national race at that level, with that level of experience.

Everybody said, "You know, she had a great speech." And we said, "Look, let's give it a few weeks to settle, and let's see what happens. You really can't judge this now. When she starts answering questions it's going to become a lot more difficult." And that's, of course, what happened.

Let's jump ahead. I believe that this race was won between September 15 and September 26. I really think this race was over after the first debate. The lines of demarcation were the first day of the Lehman Brothers collapse, the global crisis, and Senator McCain's comment that the fundamentals of the economy were strong, which just seemed completely discordant with everybody's perception of what was going on. It fed our narrative that he, like the President, was completely out of touch with the reality of the economy. We drove it hard in ads. . . .

Senator Obama had talked with [Secretary] Paulson and others the weekend before. He told us, "Something very bad is going to happen on Monday and we have to handle it very carefully. This is one place where doing the right thing is good politics. We have to do the right thing." He was very measured throughout. I think he looked very presidential, and very thoughtful, and very focused, and consistent through that nine day period.

Obviously you required a course correct for "the fundamentals of the economy are strong." When Senator McCain moved from that position to one of crisis pretty quickly, it created a sense of inconsistency. We used the word "erratic" a lot during that period. Then you suspended your campaign. Our feeling was that there was a herky-jerky nature to what was going on [in your campaign] at the time and it played well against our solidity. And I think that was reflected in the numbers.

Then came the [first] debate [September 26, 2008]. We had asked for a foreign policy debate first because we wanted to close on the economy. We thought everybody would consider foreign policy Senator McCain's strong suit. We wanted to do well in that first debate on his turf and close on our turf. [But now because of the economic crisis] the debate was going to become half economy, half foreign policy. We felt he [Senator Obama] did very well.

[One of the things the campaigns disagreed about was reflected] in the spin room afterward. A reporter said to me, "Well, Steve Schmidt said 'Obama agreed with McCain eleven times. And that shows who the leader was.'" My response was "that's the way Washington thinks about these things." I omitted the fact that you're from California. They think that if you agree on some things that there's something fundamentally weak about that. What we need is a President who can agree with people when they do agree, and contest when they don't.

We felt very good about the debate. Our dials were good. Polling on that night was good. By Tuesday we had jumped out to a pretty significant lead in these battleground states that we never released after that.

The Biden debate helped us as well. Preparing for that debate was difficult because we didn't know quite what to expect. [Michigan] Governor [Jennifer] Granholm was very effective in forecasting how Governor Palin would present herself. And Senator Biden showed a great deal of discipline in hammering that middle-class message again and again.

Through the four debates, they [Obama and Biden] each did the same thing, which was to hammer the economic and the change messages very, very hard. And each time we progressed.

When we were talking about the debates, the question was, "Do we want them to end three weeks before the election?" It's always a tough call, because if you blow [the last] debate [and it occurs late in the campaign] there's not a lot of time to recover. While we had confidence, we didn't want to take too many risks. So, we ended up [after the last debate with] three week [to go] and felt we were in a strong position [but] we had to close. We needed some intervening events.

The idea of doing a 30-minute program was to create another event that we could drive coverage with. And here having money was an obvious advantage. The program was another kind of high wire act. You could easily do a very bad 30-minute show. Mark Putnam and Jim and Davis Guggenheim put together a great piece that worked for us.

Let me say in summing this thing up, that along the way it began to occur to me that, although people said this election was going to be like '92, it was really like 1980. It was not just the end of a presidency but the end of an era, an epic in our politics. Our politics run in epics.

The year 1980 was the end of the New Deal-Great Society epoch. People were hungry for change; the economy was bad; we had problems overseas. Nothing seemed to be working. Ronald Reagan offered big change. The real question for people was, "Is he [Reagan] a safe enough choice to entrust the country to?" He answered that question in the debate with Jimmy Carter. And after that, the flood gates opened and the election was over.

I think there was a little of that here. I think people liked Obama. A lot of the things that by the end of the campaign you guys were doing, vis-à-vis some of his associations, and suggesting that he was too far left to be president didn't compute by that time because he had already established his image with people. They had seen him intensely over the course of this campaign. They knew he was a moderate personality. It just didn't compute. The debates, coupled with the financial crisis, gave people the sense of assurance they needed that this would be change, but it would be safe, as well. Here was a way to turn the page not just on the Bush Presidency, but on this era.

I don't want to be grandiose about this. We're inheriting the worst economy since the Great Depression. It's going to be very, very difficult. And I don't know what's going to happen in the future. I have great faith in this incoming president to be a great leader but he's facing problems that are incredibly difficult.

After a 28-year run, I think that the Republican project lost energy in 2008. And even though there were the Clinton years in between, just as there were the Eisenhower years during the Democratic epoch, it really was [a period] dominated by the Republican philosophy. I think people rendered a verdict on that in one of the cyclical elections in which change just overwhelms everything. I suspect that if the John McCain of 2000 were running in 2008 that he might have done better because he could have more plausibly presented himself as the candidate of change. But I don't know that he would have won.

PETER HART:

David, I'm interested in an example where all the advisors are on one side, and the candidate says, "I'm going the other way. I disagree." Was there an example of it? And what does it tell us in terms of how he'll handle the presidency?

DAVID AXELROD:

Good question. I can think of two things that are really emblematic of who he is. One was the issue of the gas tax, which came up in the primary. Both Senator McCain and Senator Clinton supported a temporary repeal of the federal gas tax [to address] high gas prices. Obama was asked about it and, without consulting anybody, said, "I'm opposed to that. We tried it in Illinois, when I was a state legislator. The oil companies filled in the gap. I don't believe people would actually see relief. I think it's a gimmick." That was one. I'm not sure. I think we actually all ultimately felt he was doing the right thing. But it was counterintuitive.

I remember talking to reporters from Washington who said "the Clinton people say you're nuts. You're going to lose the election on this. You can't be against a tax cut in the middle of a [crisis]." [But] this falls under the category "people are smarter than they get credit for." People saw it as a gimmick. And they were more interested in long term answers to the problem. On the day before the Indiana primary, we asked a straight up question. "Do you favor a temporary repeal of the gas tax?" It came out substantially against. We drove that hard [as an indicator of] his judgment.

The second was the single most impressive episode in the campaign, as far as I was concerned, and occurred [during the Reverend Wright controversy]. On a Thursday morning, these tapes of Reverend Wright burst on the scene and were being replayed constantly. Senator Obama was in Washington in the Senate that day until one in the morning. All hell was breaking loose. He was supposed to come back the next day to do some editorial boards in Chicago [about Tony Rezko].

He came back to Chicago and saw the release we wanted to put out on

Reverend Wright. He rewrote it, went off to the editorial boards without preparation, answered three hours of questions, did three cable shows on Reverend Wright, and called us that night on Friday and said, "I want to give a speech on race. I want to put this Reverend Wright thing in its proper context. By the way, I want to do it Monday or Tuesday. And I have to write it."

And we said, "Well, you know, you're campaigning all day Saturday. We've got a film shoot Sunday. You're campaigning all day in Pennsylvania on Monday. So the earliest we could it is Tuesday." He said, "Okay. Tuesday." "So, when are you gonna write it?" He said, "I know what I want to say." He dictates an outline to his speech writer—[Jon] Favreau on Saturday night. He [the writer] sends back an outline. At like 10:30 on Sunday night, Obama starts writing the speech for Tuesday. He works on it till like 3:00 in the morning. We leave at 8:00 a.m. for Pennsylvania.

So, it's not done. We campaign all day. We get back to the hotel. It's 9:30 p.m. He goes to his room. . . . I knew that he knew what he wanted to say. I woke up at 2:00 in the morning and the speech was on my Blackberry. When I read through it, I e-mailed him back and said, "This is why you should be President." He handled this thing with such grace, and such strength and such focus.

Everybody else was sort of panicky. His answer was, "You know what? I'm going to give this speech, and people will either accept it or they won't. And if they don't, then I won't be President. But at least I'll have said what needs to be said."

Peter Hart:

Is there a forecast of an Obama presidency in that?

David Axelrod:

I think what it means is he's someone who will be calm in times of great challenge and focused. I think he's someone who will be willing to do what he thinks is right for the country even if there's political risk involved. And I think that he's somebody who will be able to communicate difficult and challenging concepts and ideas to people. And I think you're going have to do that to face the problems that we're going to face in the next four and eight years.

Nicolle Wallace:

Wasn't it in that speech that he said, "I can no more disown the Reverend Wright as I can my white grandmother"? And I think it was six days before he totally disowned the Reverend Wright. Now a lot of the Clinton people at the time pointed out that this [reversal suggested] someone who was coreless, that it [his action] was pragmatic and politically expedient. We seem to be a country with a great appetite for pragmatism. Where does the core stop and the practical and the pragmatic begin? Who is he?

DAVID AXELROD:

I don't know exactly the number of days that ensued between the two.[6] But I think that without excusing Reverend Wright in his speech, he was as kind to Reverend Wright as Reverend Wright deserved. Reverend Wright [then] went on a tour over a series of days [and] became increasingly vituperative [culminating] in this odd session at the [National] Press Club. When Obama saw this, he said, "Look, this is enough. I just can't do it."

I don't know what you're asking me to describe other than to say, I think this is someone, as I said, who believes deeply in what public service is about. I think he'd be much as you described Senator McCain, willing to lose an election if he thought it meant doing something important for the country. But I do think he's pragmatic in the sense that, and he said it all the time, he is not an ideologue. He wants to solve problems. He has a great gift for not holding grudges, as you can see in how he's constructing his cabinet. He believes that people of good will can disagree, and still work together on things that they agree on. . . . I think he is someone who sets goals and objectives and then will work toward them. Whenever he dealt with difficult issues in Illinois interest legislature, and he dealt with some very difficult issues, he worked very, very assiduously to build coalitions. When he did death penalty reform in Illinois after 13 people ended up on death row who turned out to be innocent, he got prosecutors and police, defense attorneys, and civil libertarians in a room. Everybody said it was impossible to work out this legislation. It took months to do. But he found the common ground to get it done. His goal was to reform this system, and he was willing to do what was necessary to make that happen, including, and this is the other great quality that he has, to listen. He has a great capacity to listen to people. He always talks about his mother telling him, "Try and understand what the other person is thinking." And that is something that he has always done. And that is something I think he'll do as president.

At the core, he wants a good life for every family. He wants to give people a fair shake. He thinks that we're a stronger country when that happens. I don't think he's wedded to any particular device to get that done. And I think his attitude is we have to keep thinking anew. We can't reject ideas simply because they come from one side of the aisle or the other. This is going to be new for Washington.

This style of leadership is not something that they're accustomed to. It's a great experiment to see if we can restore a sense of civility and common purpose to Washington. I think the country is expecting it and those who don't make a good faith effort are doing so at their own peril.

JOEL BENENSON:

On the unattackable piece, I don't think we ever thought he [Senator Obama] was unattackable, but I think that people's appetite for certain kinds of attacks had evaporated in this election cycle.

DAVID AXELROD:

I agree with that.

JOEL BENENSON:

When people threw things out like "palling around with terrorists" or calling him a "socialist"—I think David's right—it wasn't computing, because it didn't fit with who he was. But it also didn't fit with what voters wanted to hear in this environment.

DAVID AXELROD:

Exactly right.

DAVID PLOUFFE:

Whenever Senator Clinton's [campaign] said we wanted to be President since kindergarten, or said this is the fun part of politics, we turned that against her. We could say, "We need to reject that old style of politics." We did not have that [ability] against John McCain in the beginning. When we tested [that strategy] in June and July, people wouldn't buy it. They said, "He's a different kind of politician. Okay, we'll buy that he may be too much like Bush. So, [he represents] the same old policies but [does not represent] the same old politics." That turned in August. So, while I do think there was some positive to the "celebrity" thing, some of those attacks changed people's view of McCain. They were more willing to believe that, in fact, he did engage in the same kind of politics. And we did not have that territory coming out of the primary.

DAVID AXELROD:

I would say that the financial crisis also made it harder. [Those attacks] seemed trivial in this kind of environment. But I will say, we [the Obama campaign] probably produced more negative ads against Barack Obama than you ever ran because we wanted to see how people would respond to them. [We wanted to know] how we would respond to those attacks if they came up. Although, I must say, on the whole they weren't very effective.

EMI KOLAWOLE, FACTCHECK.ORG:

I was wondering if you could speak a little bit about the message to the African American community and other minority groups. It seemed as if that issue was very strong in the beginning, particularly in Iowa. We were seeing a lot of editorials coming out, saying he wasn't black enough. And then all of a sudden, there was this groundswell. How exactly inside the campaign was that approached?

DAVID AXELROD:

Well, I have another number of reactions to that. One is I had great solicitude for him. It's hard when people are constantly peering into your soul and deciding whether you're too much, not enough, exactly who are you, and so on. That aside, he was not complaining about that.

When we started the campaign, the first analysis pushed by Mark Penn in the Clinton campaign was that we only had 30 percent of the black vote, we couldn't get African American votes. At the beginning of the race, that was true. The Clinton brand was so strong in the African American community that Barack Obama would not get black votes [because] first of all, a lot of people didn't know who he was. Second, there was I think a real apprehension in the African American community about whether America was ready to accept an African American candidate, whether this was a practical candidacy. We always knew that if we won the Iowa caucuses, in a state that was almost entirely white, that that would send a powerful signal to the African American community. That's what happened.

Our numbers began to climb exponentially after we won the Iowa caucuses. There also was the conventional wisdom after our primary that we couldn't get Hispanic votes, that we couldn't get Jewish votes, that we couldn't get Catholic votes, that we couldn't get women. And, of course, all of those [inferences] turned out to be completely ridiculous. So, I hope that part of the soul searching after this election is among the folks who get paid to write about that and talk about that. I used to do it myself. The great failing of political reporting is you sit on the back of the bus, look at what just happened and try and project forward, while looking backward. That's the wrong thing to do.

We certainly talked to the African American community directly but we didn't have a huge strategy that was different than any other strategy. Our campaign was about opportunity. It was about economic fairness and education and health care and jobs. Those issues traveled broadly. The African American community knew what his election would mean. When we started the campaign, we were in a small room, talking about whether he should run or not and Michelle Obama asked him, "What do you think you can accomplish that no one else could accomplish." And he said, "Well, one thing I know is that when I take that oath of office, there are millions of kids in this country who are going to look at themselves differently and that the world might look at us a little differently." I think that turned out to be true. But we didn't need to do anything to activate that. That was just a function of the dynamic and a healthy one.

Notes

1. John McCain said, "As you know, there's been tremendous turmoil in our financial markets and Wall Street, and it is—it's—people are frightened by these events. Our economy, I think, still the fundamentals of our economy are strong. But these are very, very difficult times. And I promise you, we will never put America in this position again. We will clean up Wall Street. We will reform government" (CNN *Newsroom* 9/15/08).

2. On September 16, 2008, McCain surrogate Carly Fiorina interviewed on the *McGraw Show*, KTRS Radio in St. Louis. Mr. Milhaven asked, "Do you think she has the experience to run a major company like Hewlett-Packard?" Carly Fiorina responded, "No, I don't, but you know what, that's not what she's running for. Running a corporation is a different set of things." The same day, Carly Fiorina appeared on MSNBC's *Andrea Mitchell Reports*. When asked about her earlier statement, Fiorina replied, "Well, I don't think John McCain could run a major corporation. I don't think Barack Obama could run a major corporation. I don't think Joe Biden could run a major corporation. But on the other hand, a major corporation is not the same as being the president or the vice president of the United States. It is a fallacy to suggest that the country is like a company" (MSNBC, http://www.msnbc.msn.com/id/21134540/vp/26741004#26741004).

3. "So we need now the Republicans to start producing some votes for us. We need the Republican nominee for president to let us know where he stands on what we should do" (Senator Harry Reid, Press Conference, Washington, D.C., 9/23/08). "If McCain doesn't come out for this, it's over," a Top House Republican tells ABC News (ABC News, Political Radar Blog 9/23/08). "I am told, Maggie, that the way that McCain got involved in this in the first place, the treasury secretary was briefing Republicans in the House yesterday. The Republican

Conference asked how many were ready to support the bailout plan. Only four of them held up their hands. Paulson then called, according to my sources, Senator Lindsay Graham, who is very close to John McCain and told him, you've got to get the people in the McCain campaign, you've got to convince John McCain to give these Republicans some political cover. If you don't do that, this whole bailout plan is going to fail. So that's how McCain apparently became involved" (Bob Schieffer, CBS, *The Early Show*, 9/25/08).

4. "The speaker had to give a partisan voice that poisoned our conference, caused a number of members who we thought we could get to go south. At the end of the day, this is not about Democrats and Republicans. It's about our economy and what's best for the American people. And regardless of what happened today, we've got—we have no choice, in my view, but to work together to try to find a solution to make sure that we save our economy and we save our constituents" (John Boehner, House Republican Leader, 9/29/08). "Right here is the reason I believe why this vote failed, and this is Speaker Pelosi's speech that frankly struck the tone of partisanship that frankly was inappropriate in this discussion" (Eric Cantor, House Minority Chief Deputy Whip, 9/29/08).

5. President Kennedy delivered his remarks at the Brandenburg Gate, June 26, 1963 (JFK Presidential Library and Museum). President Reagan delivered his remarks at the Brandenburg Gate, June 12, 1987 (Reagan Library).

6. Obama delivered his speech on race in Philadelphia, Pennsylvania, on March 18, 2008. Obama formally denounced Wright's inflammatory remarks on April 29, 2008.

Chapter 4
The Role of Polling

Bill McInturff

Bill McInturff is a partner and co-founder of Public Opinion Strategies, a leading national political and public affairs survey research firm which represents 19 U.S. senators, eight governors, and over 50 members of the House. He is actively engaged in American politics, conducting national survey research on behalf of the Republican Governors Association. Most recently, he served as the lead pollster for John McCain 2008. McInturff has conducted groundbreaking research on Medicare reform, juvenile justice reform, genetic testing, school choice, tort reform and health care policy. Previously he managed campaigns at the local, congressional and presidential levels and held senior positions with the Republican national party committees.

We all need to remember that in July 2007 the McCain campaign was dead as dead can be. By August there were literally 28 staffers. I was asked to brief the field staff. Where there were about 1,000 people in the Barack Obama campaign, the McCain field staff in March was 50 people. Here is a survey we did in May 2007.

This is a powerful chart. It was the chart that drove the rest of the race [in the primaries] but unfortunately not the chart used in the beginning. In the beginning there was an obsession with [the prospect of] a McCain/Rudy Giuliani race. And my point was "not on our planet." The two finalists are not going to be John McCain and Rudy Giuliani. They exist in the same space.

I think that the attempt to make John the inevitable Republican nominee would have worked had Giuliani not been in the race. John would have been at 38 percent in every poll, and that campaign would have worked. But McCain and Giuliani were splitting 38 percent of the Republican primary. Romney was holding 25 percent. The rest of the Republican field was more conservative than Romney. The undecided voters were the single most conservative part of the party. The reason Romney could have been the nominee is [that] he was sitting right in the middle of the Republican electorate. It was a lot easier for Romney to move over and grab those voters than it would be for John.

CHART 7. PRIMARY ELECTION TARGET SEGMENTS

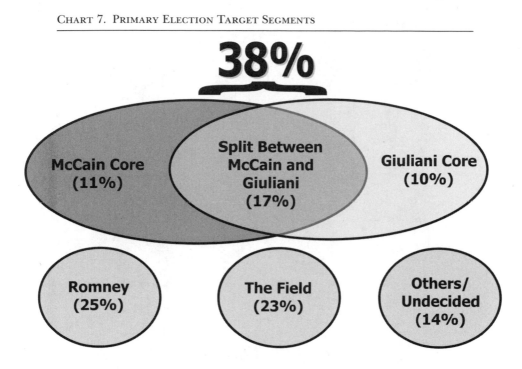

By the way, things [in the McCain campaign] weren't in good shape. Romney was advertising like crazy. We're on the telephone in late May 2007 saying, "We need a million dollars of TV to have some kind of response." The campaign handlers responded, "Maybe after the June 30th filing we can have money for TV." We got off the phone and said, "Let me see. We've just raised $90 million and there's not a million dollars left in cash to go on TV in May? This is not good."

In July the press kept saying, "When's he going to quit?" I said, "Here's what would make him stop: rigor mortis or when somebody has enough delegates to be nominated." It isn't just his biography. Five and a half years of torture. The guy moved to Arizona and ran against the three single most popular Republicans in the district. He spent 18 months six hours a day door-to-door campaigning.

Now I don't know if you've ever done door-to-door work. Six hours a day for 18 months. He met 25,000 primary voters in person. That's how he won the congressional open seat primary. I said, "When he has no money left, he will be dragging the bus with his teeth. He'll be campaigning door-to door in New Hampshire. He will not stop."

It was a remarkable effort on his part. It was a remarkable effort on Steve [Schmidt] and Rick Davis's part to hang in there. People left in

Bill McInturff

Washington. [But] there was really not a single finance committee member, a state chairman, a volunteer chairman, a county chairman, or any of the other key volunteers who left. They all stayed in the campaign. There are two things it takes to be president. You have to have the capacity to drag a dead campaign on the strength of your personality, which is what Senator Obama did in 2007, 30 points behind. And you have to have people walk through fire for you because they care about you.

My friend, Peter Hart, said the zeitgeist of this election is "change, open, accountable, transparent and not like Bush." He would joke, "That's going to be Hillary Clinton and Romney? They don't fit that zeitgeist." . . .

Since 1952 we've had monthly polling by the Michigan consumer sentiment folks. I've looked at generations of political results based on consumer confidence. We have the worst economic climate ever measured since World War II. There've been three times in American history where that barometer's dropped below 60. We're in one of the three.

The other two were in 1974 and '75, which, you know, wiped out a

CHART 8. CAMPAIGN SPENDING IN STATES THAT FLIPPED FROM RED TO BLUE

State	Amount McCain Spent	Amount Obama Spent	Difference (McCain-Obama)
Nevada	$5.6m	$7.9m	-$2.3m
Colorado	$8.2m	$10.2m	-$2.0m
New Mexico	$3.1m	$3.3m	-$0.2m
Virginia	$7.5m	$23.8m	-$16.3
North Carolina	$3.5m	$10.7m	-$7.2m
Florida	$8.3m	$36.7m	-$28.4
Ohio	$14.5m	$21.4m	-$6.9m
Indiana	$0.4m	$11.8m	-$11.4m
Iowa	$5.1m	$3.6m	+$1.5m
Total	$56.2m	$129.4m	-$73.2m

Republican presidency[1] and in '79 and '80, which wiped out Jimmy Carter.[2] In September and October [the country experienced] the single largest monthly drop in that measure in 50 years.

When the party in power wins, the Michigan consumer sentiment index is at least 96. The three times it's been in the 70s, the party in power has lost: Jimmy Carter, Gerry Ford, and George H. W. Bush in '92. In October [2008] the number was 58. In other words, there's not a number like this. When you look at those numbers, you conclude that we're going to lose the election. So, to work against this environment and not lose the election, what would you do that's riskier than you'd ever thought possible?

Here is spending by state according to *National Journal.* It's not just on air, it's state spending. Note the states that switched from red to blue. The Democrats have a little bit of a spending advantage: $24 million in Virginia. $36 million in Florida. And $21 million in Ohio. In Indiana, $11 million. We're $73 million down in spending.

This chart reflects the answers to the question, "Do you remember seeing more ads from Barack Obama, John McCain or both?" You didn't have to pick one. You could say "both."

In my career, if you said "Please tell me where you've got a chart where someone's got a 64 to 12 advantage on recalled advertising," I

CHART 9. OBAMA'S MASSIVE SPENDING ADVANTAGE CHANGED THIS CAMPAIGN

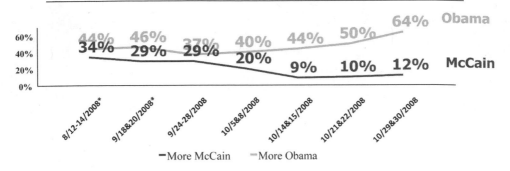

don't have charts like this. If somebody's this far behind or ahead, no one does daily tracking. You don't have charts that look like this in what is ostensibly a competitive campaign.

Steve's and my joke in the campaign was, "Through September we had the most unpopular president in polling history. We had an unpopular war. The economy was lousy with 75 percent [saying the country was on the] 'wrong track' and we were winning."

So, what did we do? What we did was move wrong track into the '90s. Steve said to me one morning, "Have you ever seen a number like this?" I said, "Steve, I'm a veteran pollster. Of course. Bulgaria. 1992." So, if you're a Russian breakaway republic in 1992, you can have 91 percent wrong track. It exists. It's happened before in the world. Then Rick said, "Well, hell, maybe we should move to Bulgaria. Start running campaigns there. They're used to this kind of stuff."

At 90 percent wrong track, lots of things start cracking. You can explain the action of the Republicans by using game theory. They all think they're casting a safe vote individually by voting against the bailout. Except, guess what happens? They tube the package. They take the hit and it goes on for eight more days.

Then, after they finally vote for that terrible bill, the market drops. So, instead of being a bad one-week story where you hope you can contain the damage and go back to a campaign, it becomes two and a half or three weeks plus the damage. What happened [as a result] is a shift in that huge part of the Republican constituency [consisting of] white, college educated guys. We had been winning fairly comfortably with white, college guys. Then their stock market portfolios dropped about 1,800 points over about two months and they said, "That's it. Now I'm afraid. I'm getting affected by the economy." McCain won white, college guys by single digits in this election.

September 15 is a killer for the following reasons. First and most important it fed into a narrative which is, "That's it. I've had it. The Republicans and George Bush have helped the rich. This doesn't work. Everything's broken." And by the way, that's a rational response.

It had other real consequences. We stopped having a campaign. The daily press report wasn't reporting, "He said. She said. Back. Forth. This story. This story." [Instead the story was]: "Today America's economy is falling apart. Here's how awful everything is. Here's the candidates' reaction to it."

And you're a sidebar. Despite Republicans liking to claim "press bias," who among you can call up a reporter and say, "You should get rid of those banner headlines about how awful the economy is." It was a huge story. It was the most important story. And it's an important story that blew us off the front pages.

And what's the other consequence? The Obama campaign was able to spent $105 million in two weeks in October, meaning you had the money to be heard above that din when we were stuck in it.

Then here's the last thing. People say, "Why didn't you run a campaign against Obama?" We had a campaign against Obama. It started September 24, with the Chicago ad.[3] That's the start of what was going to be a 6- or 7-week narrative saying, "He's not quite the guy you think he is." "He's not quite the guy you think he is. He's not quite ready."[4]

We tested months of positive McCain stuff and it didn't move a single number. To the extent that we had a chance, this race had to be about Senator Obama. We presumed that he's (Obama's) going to be great here, great here, great here. So, if you make the race about Senator Obama, what do you have to do? What people said is, "Who the heck is this guy? I never even heard of him six months ago. Ever heard of this guy? Is he really going to be president? What's he really done? Is he experienced enough?"

There're a lot of fundamental questions. You can feed into that by saying, "In fact, there's more about him you need to know. He's not the reformer you think he is. He's part of this Chicago machine. We have these concerns. Here's in fact—." We were going to start with the Chicago story, because in fact the guy did have a layer of protection. If you started with the issues, people said, "No, that doesn't fit. Doesn't fit. Doesn't fit. That's not the guy I'm seeing."

We had to raise fundamental questions about the guy they were seeing. We ran that ad the day Lehman [Brothers crashed]. Instead [of the press focusing] on "celebrity two" and having five days of the Chicago story, the story that day is the collapse of Lehman and what's happening to the economy. And our typical campaign stuff gets blown off the air. . . .

We would desperately try to aggregate enough money to stay competitive in advertising. We'd be only $8 million behind this week or only $4 million behind when the Obama campaign would buy $10 million of 2-minute spots. If you want to know what the key markets were, it isn't hard. [Look at the polling]. The campaign would say to me, "Bill, what do you think he bought?" And I would say, "Well, I tell you where they bought. They bought Orlando." And they said, "Gee, Bill, that's exactly the markets they bought." It's not a secret why they dropped $10 million into those markets. Those markets were the key to who's left in this election.

And by the way—if you're the typical American voter saying, "Who's running a negative campaign?"—Barack Obama's got $10 million of positive stuff on there for two minutes and he's fabulous on film. Then he could also be running this "let's rip your heart out on the health care tax ad." So, they could sustain three things at once where we're trying with those horrible hybrid ads to have anything to say. . . .

I had my own focus group at home. I have two boys, 17 and 13. Teenage boys don't watch TV; they watch sports. We live in northern D.C. and the first thing they started saying in October was, "I never see John McCain. I see Barack Obama all day long."

Then it got a little bit better. They said, "I see John McCain, but I don't understand what those spots mean? Who are the liberal people and what's that got to do with Barack Obama?"

Steve asked, "Does anyone think this hybrid stuff actually helps? Why are we doing this? This is awful." We had two awful choices: these horrible ads or giving up any control we have of the campaign. We decided that the hybrid ads were so horrible that we'd give up control and give them [the RNC] the $30 million. Then we could at least run our 30-second ads and we finally had something semicoherent from the RNC on the air.

God bless Joe Biden. Biden says, "Of course, he's going to be tested. Everybody knows that."[5] [That admission] meant we could put on the air something that people found convincing. Joe Biden's not a Republican and Joe Biden says he's going to be tested. Voters also found convincing that Barack Obama had said he wanted to share the wealth. [As a result], after having lost the tax message, we got it back. And we kind of re-stabilized the campaign.

Then my 13-year-old came to me and said, "Don't we want terrorists to be afraid of the American president? Because if the terrorists aren't afraid of the American president, it's very unsafe. So, if Barack Obama's vice president thinks he's going to be tested, isn't that unsafe for America?" And I said, "Yes! Yes!"

My 13-year-old finally understood the last 10 days of advertising in the campaign. He would say, "I'm worried about Barack Obama because, why would we let somebody operate as a doctor if he hasn't ever been a doctor before?" He was replaying the RNC "experience" ad.

I'm thinking, "We finally have something on the air a 13-year-old could understand." And by the way, it was a good measure because when my 13-year-old understood the advertising, our verbatim—[showed that] somebody else understood them [as well].

[We have a powerful measure that asks based on what] you're seeing recently, are you more favorable or less favorable about John McCain and Barack Obama? During those two to two and a half weeks in October where all this stuff was coming together, we were being shredded. We were drifting in state after state to numbers like 13 percent more positive about McCain with 48, 51, 54 more negative. If Barack Obama's a positive, and you get to minus 25, you start cracking.

In the last week or 10 days, we were away from the debates, away from Barack Obama. We had something coherent on the air. We had something to say. And McCain's favorables started going back up. Our net, in terms of "are you more or less favorable to McCain" starts going up. Our favorables go up. Palin's go up. Barack Obama never made big time negative, [but] we started at least getting in the ballgame. When General Powell endorsed Barack Obama that was the low point of our [battleground] tracking. We went from minus five to literally minus 11 after the weekend of the Powell endorsement. Then we went from minus 11, minus 9, minus 8, minus 6. You could see [that we were] getting back in the ballgame across these battleground states I just hoped that we'd be within margin of error, that we were making progress in the campaign. And then I think people heard that in our last weekend. On a Monday, we pop back to minus 4, then minus 6. Our last track on Monday across these states was minus 6.

What is my secret hope? I don't ask for much. If the American economy is going to collapse, fine, but please do it in December. Couldn't we just please, God, have done it in December? I would have liked to have run this campaign without a collapsing American economy and with something like equal money.

If in May somebody had said, "Look, the RNC will take in $175 million in September online," if someone had said to me that that was really ever going to happen, can you imagine if we'd had, like, $200 million, $250 million the RNC raised online that we could have spent rationally? It would have been a very different campaign. I do believe that without the collapse of the American economy and [with] something like equal money the result wouldn't have changed, but I think it would've been a very long night.

A general election presidential campaign teaches you how fundamentally different it is to run for president than to run even for governor of a huge state, or any other race. You start thinking about your responsibility to the country in a way that means you do not talk about Reverend Wright if you're John McCain. Because, you think, "I could be President of the United States of America. How could I lead this country had I run that campaign?" And it means that when, as Steve is joking, every smart person who tells you, "No, no, America's going to blow up and it's going to be like the depression unless you do this by Monday," you don't [rely on] your normal instincts. [The candidates say] "The two of us have to do the responsible, rational thing because someone's going to be president and they can't inherit this."

JON CARSON:

Why did you pick Michigan to pull out of?

BILL McINTURFF:

We were down 16 in Michigan by late September. We also had a candidate who said to people in the primary, "the jobs aren't coming back."[6] We don't have enough money, we're 12 or 15 down, [and the economy in Michigan is bleak]. It's horrifying. They're stuck in their houses. They can't move. And John said, "These jobs aren't coming back." How hard is it to run an ad campaign [against us] where you say, "Well, let's see what John says about your state?" "Jobs aren't coming back." And [running there would] cost millions and millions and millions of dollars. If you said in late September, with the money we had left and the barrage that was hitting us, "Are we better off trying to go to a state that has a much smaller African American population unlike Detroit, in a better economic situation like Wisconsin and Pennsylvania," I'd take my chances in Wisconsin and Pennsylvania rather than trying to believe we'll ever have money to compete in Michigan given what our candidate said in the state. There's not a single day I blush about begging people to get out of Michigan. The bad choice was running the first two, two and a half weeks of advertising in Michigan trying to see if it could ever get better. Getting out in September I don't regret at all.

Joel Benenson

Joel Benenson is founding partner of Benenson Strategy Group, a New York-based strategic research and polling firm. Benenson was the lead pollster for the Obama campaign, conducting battleground polling during the campaign and playing an active role in debate preparation. His other clients include Senators Robert

Menendez and Frank Lautenberg and Mayors Cory Booker of Newark and Gavin Newsom of San Francisco. During the last two cycles he has also polled for the DCCC, helping the Democrats pick up 16 seats from Republicans. Since 2004 he has done extensive research for Service Employees International Union, the nation's largest union, on the economic lives of swing voters.

David Axelrod said correctly that coming out of the 50 states we had certain advantages. We did know that the fundamentals of the campaign we were running were pretty much established. That being said, we never ran in the general election what you'd call a traditional benchmark poll.

We did know that we had to make some adjustments; we knew that the electorate that we were looking at was different from a Democratic primary electorate. The people we might need to persuade would conceivably be different. We were certainly running against a different opponent in John McCain who many Democrats thought would be the most formidable opponent we faced. We did feel like we were playing catch up. We had an enormous amount of work to do.

David Plouffe always jokes that one mistake we made was too much polling. He just said it to me again. But, we knew we had a lot of work to do as we shifted to a general election and not much time to do it. Since we didn't want to be perceived as polling in a general election before we were out of the primaries, we really didn't poll until late May. In May we did the only national poll we did. The rest of the season [was focused on] the 22 states that are on the map.

That got whittled down to 18 states very quickly. But, we didn't wait for all our data to come in. In this national poll we really wanted to decide how we come out of the box here.

We had two concerns in May as we looked ahead and asked, "What do we need to get out of our polling?" They both related to John McCain. One was the image that we believed he would have as a change agent. This was our territory. It was something that we thought people believed about him. The press certainly wrote about it. The other was the degree to which this guy who had this unbelievable biography that everybody knew, a war hero, could make the Commander in Chief argument in a much more compelling way than we faced in a Democratic primary. We would have to deal with that.

A few surprises came out of that first poll [as well as] a lot of good insights that actually held us in good stead during the course of the entire campaign. But, it also gave us a pretty good sense that our overall message was exactly where we needed to be.

We ended the primaries with this myth that the Clinton campaign had spent weeks spinning about all the groups that we were weak with. It

CHART 10. BATTLEGROUND MAP

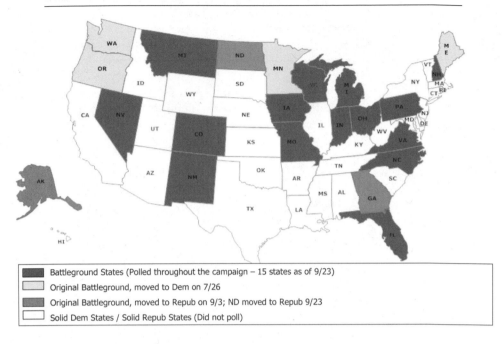

Battleground States (Polled throughout the campaign – 15 states as of 9/23)

Original Battleground, moved to Dem on 7/26

Original Battleground, moved to Repub on 9/3; ND moved to Repub 9/23

Solid Dem States / Solid Repub States (Did not poll)

wasn't just that we won those by Election Day. In this first poll, [we looked at] the very groups that we were told we were weak with: senior women, non-college women, Hispanics, union households, and Catholics who were always a historically swing voter group. We were strong with all those groups, save Catholics with whom we were competitive. We were down only two points.

On the other hand, we owned people with college degrees throughout the primary. Suddenly we were in a fight or were weak with them. Young men, 18–44, we thought we owned the youth vote. But, young men were very late in coming to us.

When we looked at the data we saw a mirror image of what we had believed.

The second surprise, and this goes to one of the fundamental principles: we discovered in May that we were much better defined with the electorate than John McCain was. On every attribute we tested, except those that related to John McCain's biography, we were ahead of him.

McCain was very low on all attributes and, in particular, was not perceived as a change agent. If you look at just those bars in front of you, the [black] bars reflect Obama's rating on the attribute. The [gray] bar, McCain's. This is not a head-to-head test. They were both rated evenly

CHART 11. SHIFTING THE MINDSET—DEMOCRATIC PRIMARY DYNAMICS DO NOT HOLD IN THE GENERAL ELECTION

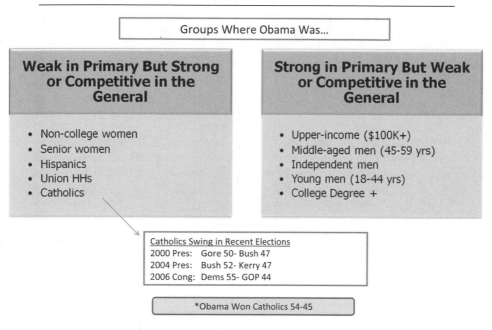

Groups Where Obama Was...

Weak in Primary But Strong or Competitive in the General

- Non-college women
- Senior women
- Hispanics
- Union HHs
- Catholics

Strong in Primary But Weak or Competitive in the General

- Upper-income ($100K+)
- Middle-aged men (45-59 yrs)
- Independent men
- Young men (18-44 yrs)
- College Degree +

Catholics Swing in Recent Elections
2000 Pres: Gore 50- Bush 47
2004 Pres: Bush 52- Kerry 47
2006 Cong: Dems 55- GOP 44

*Obama Won Catholics 54-45

CHART 12. OBAMA CLEARLY IDENTIFIED AS CHANGE AGENT

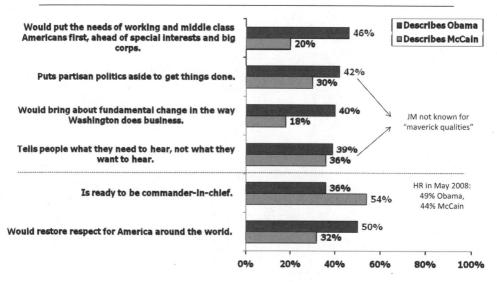

- Describes Obama
- Describes McCain

Would put the needs of working and middle class Americans first, ahead of special interests and big corps. — 46% / 20%

Puts partisan politics aside to get things done. — 42% / 30%

Would bring about fundamental change in the way Washington does business. — 40% / 18%

Tells people what they need to hear, not what they want to hear. — 39% / 36%

Is ready to be commander-in-chief. — 36% / 54%

Would restore respect for America around the world. — 50% / 32%

JM not known for "maverick qualities"

HR in May 2008: 49% Obama, 44% McCain

0%   20%   40%   60%   80%   100%

in May. And on the top half of this chart were all the attributes we used as our "essential change attributes." They related to putting the middle class first ahead of special interests, putting partisan politics aside, the basic attribute on bringing fundamental change to Washington and our surrogate for straight talk, telling people what they need to know, not what they want to hear. Not only did we have commanding leads on those change attributes, except for straight talk where we were at parity, but we had double digit leads on all of them.

When we looked at the ones that related to the world at large, foreign affairs, the commander in chief territory, we were only down 18 points to John McCain on who was ready to be commander in chief in May 2008. I say "only down 18 points," because it sounds like a big number. But, there were two takeaways that we got from that. We believed at this point that this would be a high point for McCain. Everybody knew him. They knew he was a decorated war hero. And we believed it would be a low point for Obama.

But second, what the small print says on the left, we were ahead by 5 points in this first national poll, 49–44. So we're lagging on the commander in chief attribute [but ahead in the horse race], a piece of data that defies conventional wisdom. All those thinkers tell you, "Oh, every presidential election is about who's the better commander and chief." Well, it isn't.

You have to clear a threshold with voters. You have to persuade them that you are up to the job, and that you are ready for it. We believed that over the course of this campaign we could actually persuade voters that Barack Obama was ready to be commander and chief. Two things were behind that. One of them is that last attribute on the chart, is, "would restore respect for America around the world."

There we had an 18-point lead over John McCain. So even though he owned the commander in chief image, the other thing that was nagging the American electorate was our image around the world. They think we needed to restore respect for our image. We had a very commanding lead on that. That gave us a lot of confidence going into that first foreign policy debate.

One thing a lot of us internally knew was that in Chicago Barack Obama did pay a lot of attention to some of the intricacies on NATO. He's been a student of foreign affairs. When you sat in a room with him, even from my first exposure to him, which was in early '07, the breadth of his knowledge about foreign affairs was striking. We believed going into that first debate that if we held our ground with McCain, if we came out of that first debate even on foreign policy, if our headline was "Obama goes toe to toe with McCain on foreign policy," it was pretty much game over.

Joel Benenson

We also knew the same thing that the Republicans did. They were up against a mammoth task. In this poll we created a basic contrast on eight different things, not mentioning a candidate's name and asking who you are more likely to vote for. For example one question asked about a candidate who "supports changing course from Bush policies or supports continuing them." On Iraq, "one strongly supports the war, and stays there as long as it takes to win. The other opposes the war, and says begin a reasonable withdrawal." On each of these metrics, it wasn't just that Bush was negative, but that his policies were negative. It wasn't just that the Republicans had all that baggage but because of the Faustian bargains David [Axelrod] pointed to John McCain implicitly became inextricably linked to Bush's policies, on the war, and on the economy. It also fit into a sense that he was out of touch, which in September we were able to exploit, particularly with [McCain's] comment on the economy on the day Lehman Brothers collapsed.

The other thing we tested in this first poll was a very simple construct. We basically wanted to boil down the race to one thing that mattered

most to people. . . . We came out of this first poll with three-quarters of
the electorate telling us that this [election] was going to be about fixing
the economy and bringing about change in Washington. We knew in
our gut that the economy was a big issue. We had just gone through a
primary, where we had fought that. But what these data allowed us to do
was not get distracted by Senator McCain's emphasis on commander in
chief. We knew we didn't have to push back on it. We knew we had time
to clear the threshold and not get sucked into that game, and continue
fighting on our turf.

We had one source of concern regarding the economy. There's a
breakout group of voters we called "up for grabs" that was identified in
this poll as a swing group we were going to go after. These were the most
persuadable people. They also aligned very much on the economy and
change in Washington. In fact, a lot of our other data showed that they
were more driven [than non-"up for grabs" voters] by the economy and
a desire for change in Washington.

Among voters overall who said the election was about who had the
best plan to fix the economy, we had a 26-point lead in the horse race.
Among the "up for grabs" voters who said the economy was the most
important thing, we were basically dead even back in May. We also knew,
by the way, that even though we led on the attribute "who could best fix
the economy," we weren't high enough. We had a 32 percent rating.
McCain was at 19. We felt this was up for grabs. We had to make sure we
staked out ownership of the economy, and not let him get his footing
on that turf.

We used four different metrics to classify people. They ended up in
three groups. We played with about twenty different combinations:
Obama base, McCain base, and "up for grabs" voters.

And the four metrics were related to partisan identification, who you
were voting for, stated voting patterns, how often you say you vote for
someone in the other party, and your certainty of vote in this election.
These [up for grabs] voters were not all undecided, but they were much
more undecided than the general election. We felt we could win them
right from the start, because they were highly independent, placed a
heavy emphasis on the economy and on ending the war in Iraq, in particular. They also showed a more populist strain. These were the folks
who were rebelling against the dominance of lobbyists and special interests in Washington.

In June, right after this poll, before we get our feet on the ground,
and are able to get to some of the other research that we wanted to do
for the general election, we're caught up in this moment where, rightly
described, the McCain campaign took very direct action on drilling.

In our polling we saw the same things everybody saw: by two to one,

CHART 13. DRILLING—VOTERS WANTED ACTION BUT KNEW IT WASN'T THE ONLY ANSWER

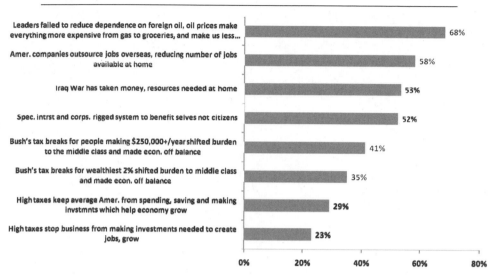

People supported drilling. But everywhere else we tested it, if you look at the bottom, we asked people, "What were the most important immediate steps? Was it to increase drilling for oil and natural gas in the United States, and off the coastal shores, or take immediate steps to reduce demand through conservation initiatives, such as fuel efficiency standards for cars, trucks, and investments in research?"

People were hungry for action. Gas prices were going up. But that really didn't supplant what they saw as the number one economic issue dragging us down, and the number one national security issue, and that was our dependence on foreign oil.

We knew we had to push back hard on drilling and concede it at a certain point but really place the emphasis on long-term solutions. If you go back and look at transcripts, Senator McCain would talk about it [long-term solutions], but it was a throwaway line in the speech. He'd say, "And of course we have to do wind, and solar, and nuclear."

Other than the attacks on Obama for being opposed to those things, which by the way, Senator Obama never was, [Senator McCain] really never gave a full throated defense of the rest of his energy plan during the course of the general. "Drill baby drill" became the rallying cry at the rallies, which was really not enough for the voters. They really understood, to their credit, that problems like health care [and] energy were related to our economic struggles, but they were problems of long term making that were going to require complex solutions, not quick fixes.

In May, we asked people what were the factors contributing to the economic downturn. The least important factors were high income taxes on individuals or high taxes on businesses. People were much more inclined to blame our energy dependence for our economic downturn, outsourcing of American jobs, the war in Iraq, by the way, sapping money that we needed at home, and the influence of special interests.

So, as McCain relied on what I would call predictable Republican rhetoric about taxes, I really believed it as another signal that he was a little bit out of touch with people, or a little bit tone deaf to where they were on the fundamentals of our economy, frankly, to use that phrase, if I may. They saw much bigger problems at work there. And the other thing is that these were not issues on their own. They were inextricably linked not just to our economic plight but to what people thought was wrong with Washington.

If you recall, Senator Obama repeatedly said, "For decades we've been talking about these problems, and doing nothing." It was an implicit indictment on Washington because they were all part of a package.

Nicolle said the economy was issue one, two, three, four, and five, and it was all the economy. The fact is, we looked at this in July, and we looked at it again. The economy was unquestionably the dominant issue, and we were going to focus our campaign on it in the fall. But we also knew that the war in Iraq repeatedly came up as the number two issue. It came up, by the way, when we wanted to look at why people thought Bush had failed on the economy. Iraq had distracted his [President Bush's] attention from problems at home and had sapped resources as well. So, when we were going into the debates, we were comfortable with our terrain in Iraq as an economic issue. It also helped, you do catch luck along the way, that Iraq had a 79 billion dollar surplus announced in mid-September, and we were able to link the 10 billion a month with that.

Right before the debates, we also tested our push back against Senator McCain's argument that the surge had worked. And we had an 18-point lead on our argument about the surge versus McCain's. It was pretty staggering. If you remember Senator Obama's argument on that was, "Yes, the surge had worked to reduce violence but it hadn't changed the fundamental fact that six years later we're still mired in Iraq, we're still spending 10 billion dollars a month, and we're still not making the Iraqis take responsibility for their own country."

So we went into the foreign policy debate which was still going to be spent [primarily] on foreign policy feeling pretty confident about our ability to lean into Iraq as a contrast that we wanted to have with Senator McCain in that debate. We weren't turning away from it.

I'm going to touch on Palin briefly, and then wrap up. The bottom of this slide shows the horse race flow.

CHART 14. THE PALIN EFFECT

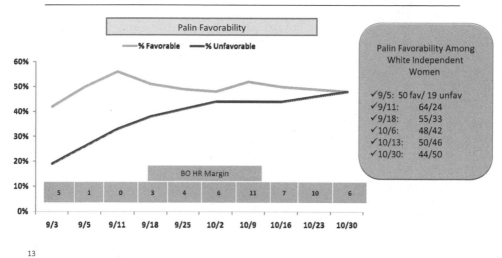

13

We never saw the McCain camp take any more than a one-point lead, and it was really a two-point in our battleground states, by the way. Also, in our battleground states we knew historically that the Democratic candidate ran about two to three points better nationally, than in the 15 or 16 battleground states. But you see Palin's favorability go through that. First, we never made the choice about Palin. If you go back and look at our campaign, we said almost nothing about Sarah Palin. We really held our powder. We wanted to make it John McCain, and John McCain's decision making. The word "erratic" was something that we applied to this as well.

We did think that Governor Palin would deliver a good performance [in the vice presidential debate]. Our mission with Biden during debate prep was not to even engage her. Senator Biden's mission was to defend Barack Obama and draw the contrast with John McCain. You know, don't get caught up in anything with Palin at that debate.

When we looked at the voters, the movement because of Palin occurred primarily among white independent women and younger women. We did feel that when we focused more on the economy, we would win those women back. We got them back during the economic crisis and before the Palin debate. The Katie Couric interviews, and the Tina Fey stuff, I believe, did some damage, and really dragged down Governor Palin's image as being ready for the job. And that started showing up in polls reporting [the perception] that she wasn't ready to be vice president.

While I think she gave a very good performance in the debate, the media threshold for her was "she didn't trip over anything, she delivered her sound bites. She got off a couple of good lines." But because of the intervening dynamics, I think that she had a different threshold in that debate. She had to convince people in that debate that she was up for the job of being Vice President. She didn't clear that threshold in those 90 minutes. Admittedly, [doing so] was a mammoth task.

Similarly, in the debates with John McCain, we believed that we had to provide a sense of command and control. We had to come off as presidential and show that we're as presidential as this guy. We thought McCain had to demonstrate to the American people that he could bring change. We never got a sense [that he focused on that] in those debates. That's why I think we came out of the debates feeling like we had pretty much wrapped it up.

In that May poll, we mapped out a model for the election [outcome] of 53–47 percent. Now I'm not going to sit here and tell you that I was predicting 53–47. In fact, in the first presentation [of those data], I said, "Look, I think it's more likely we get to 51 than 53 but we have to push our goals for a 53 percent target to make sure we have enough of a buffer to win the election, and win the electoral vote."

We had targets for 12 different groups. With independents we needed to gain six points. We set a goal of 52. We ended with 52. Among men, we needed to get to 50. We got to 49. With women we needed to get to 56, and we got to 56. With white women, we needed to get to 47, and we got to 46.

So, at the end of the day, we were able to hit some pretty big targets. We fell down a little bit among white voters, but we really picked up by outperforming among Latinos, which, you recall, were one of those groups we weren't supposed to do well with, if you listened to folks at the end of the primary.

PETER HART:

If you told me at any point in my life that one candidate's representative would be sitting here complaining about the huge spending advantage that the other had, and told me it was a Republican candidate doing the complaining, I wouldn't have believed it. What brought about this historic reversal?

BILL MCINTURFF:

When you read the Ten Commandments, in the small print it said, Republicans were given more money. Okay, that's what I thought. I thought it was part of the Ten Commandments. The point is, and this is something

CHART 15. MODELING THE VOTE TO 53%: FOCUS ON INDEPENDENTS AND
SUBURBANITES

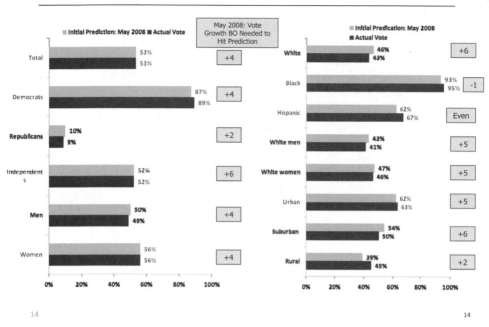

that Speaker Gingrich talks about, new technologies create tidal waves
that change history. We have a new technology in the internet. It gets rid
of all those years of our building our small [mail-based] donor base. This
was an extraordinary election, in which the level of interest was beyond
anything ever measured. People cared passionately.

We had very exciting candidates. People wanted to participate. The
viewership of the convention speeches and debates was extraordinary.
They had technology where you got interested and boom you give
money. To Peter's broader question, the Democrats [are now] starting
with literally millions of donors, millions of people on list.

For an administration to have the capacity to sell a legislative package
and create a legislative agenda is an incredible powerful starting point.
Access to technology combined with an unusually important election
and a very exciting candidate has transformed American politics. I don't
know for how long but [for now] it's a unique advantage.

PETER HART:

Why couldn't John McCain use that same technology to do the same
thing?

Bill McInturff:

What did we raise in the RNC, $200 million in two months—$150 million? The honest other part of the story is, in September and October the RNC raised something like $250 million. If anyone had a clue that that was feasible or possible, who in their right mind would have taken the 87 million? It just happened too late for us to have a clue it was going to happen, and [by] then we were stuck with the system.

Joel Benenson:

While people were very engaged, there was an enthusiasm gap that was very real because of the historic nature of Senator Clinton's run, and Barack Obama's run, and because of the kind of campaign that was set up from the start to bring people in. Back in May, our "very favorables" were twice as high as John McCain's "very favorables."

We had a lot more intensity, the certainty of our vote from the start was higher. But your question goes to a broader point, and I think if we're going to admonish the talking heads in the media a bit, this election defied the conventional wisdom at so many different steps in the process, that they really ought to learn to hold their fire, and rethink what they think they know. I'm a former journalist so I can say it.

But the truth of the matter is that one of the things the money allowed us to do was to continually challenge our assumptions. If we thought we had a message that worked, and you said something different, and we wanted to make sure we were right, we could go back and test it. We had a plan that allowed us to do that. We were challenging our assumptions all the time. After so much conventional wisdom was stood on its head, they [the media talk heads] should probably hold their fire a bit.

Peter Hart:

Neither of you mentioned race at all. I'm wondering how race will affect the Obama presidency. Was there anything particular in terms of measuring that, or understanding that that you found particularly effective?

Joel Benenson:

I should probably quote David Plouffe, who often said, "The number of meetings we had where we talked about race as an issue is zero." Even in our polling and focus groups, we did very minimal probing of it. It was a reality. There are certain things you can control in a campaign and certain things you can't. President-elect Obama would say frequently,

"Look, I'm not going to win this because I'm African American, and I'm not going to lose because I'm African American."

We did want to raise the stakes at our convention. We believed that this was a mammoth election, and we did want to raise the stakes for voters, and make them think this was an extremely important election because we believed that that accrued to our advantage. The voters always show how smart they are. They understand the stakes are high. They know, as Bill said, that this is not a problem of President-elect Obama's making, and I think there's also a desire for him to succeed. I don't want to say we're in a post racial period. That would be naïve. But I think the stakes that are at play for America at large are much greater than some of those more narrow issues. I could be wrong.

BILL MCINTURFF:

. . . We did ask people how much they'd heard about Reverend Wright. That story happened in March or April. You could sit in a focus group in October and people would recount the entire story about what he'd [Rev. Wright] said, and he [Senator Obama] was in the pew, and he [Rev. Wright] did the baptism. Even without it ever being mentioned in the campaign, it was a powerful subtext. For people for whom that was a concern that was not new information, whether or not we ever chose to talk about it.

JOEL BENENSON:

And a majority of Americans felt that he had dealt with it very well back in March.

KATHLEEN HALL JAMIESON:

To the Republicans, are there any other things you wish you could have changed?

BILL MCINTURFF:

In October, we had a line which promised you the next four years will not be like the last eight years. I wish we said that at the convention. I wish the convention speech had been sharper. Someone mentioned the 2006 speech that John did. That is one of the things I wish would have shifted.

KATHLEEN HALL JAMIESON:

What polling did you do on Senator McCain's age? What did it tell you, and what if any effect did that have on what you did in the campaign?

JOEL BENENSON:

Back in May we threw in [the questions] "Did people think Senator McCain was too old? Did they think Senator Obama was too young?" Both of those got very low ratings. We really never paid attention to it again. It's one of those things that's a fact out there, that existed. We didn't think we needed a poll on it. People knew he was 72 years old. That was coming back loud and clear.

The only other thing we threw into the attributes at that point, and it didn't stay in our attribute battery, was, "has the energy and the vigor to meet the demands of presidency." There was a big difference there. And what it told us was, just leave it alone.

ANITA DUNN:

It's already there.

JOEL BENENSON:

It was already there. There was a disparity between Obama and McCain on that. His task was going to have to be to show he had the vigor to meet the demands of the job and we never had to talk about it.

BILL MCINTURFF:

One time I said to John, "your mother sure was beautiful." And he said, "I like to say 'My mother is beautiful,' Bill." And I'm thinking, "Oh my God, I've stepped in it again. She must be like 94." And then he says, "She just bought a BMW convertible in Germany, and she and her twin are flying over to pick it up, and drive around Europe."

If you work for John, you don't worry about energy and vitality, because you've been close to the guy. Steve said," In every commercial, he's eating donuts in the straight talk express in a lounge chair. He looks like he's in a frickin' Barcalounger."

JOEL BENENSON:

On his way to Atlantic City.

BILL McINTURFF:

He [Steve] said, "Does anyone really think that's helping us?" And "If not that, then he's sitting in the airplane being interviewed." And so, we had to change the optics of him on the road [and put] younger people around him, [and the like].

It's the same thing as race. John's 72. . . . We were leaking water in ten different valves, and you're trying to shut the first seven valves that are the most rational to get that water to stop, before you can get to the last. All day long you're trying to fix the water leaks. You run out of time and money. In the scheme of what we had to fix, being too close to Bush, and the economy and all the rest, we had [a great deal] to get fixed way before we worried about John's age.

Notes

1. In the fourth quarter of 1974, the CSI index dropped to 59.5.
2. In the second quarter of 1980, the CSI index dropped to 54.4.
3. "Chicago Machine" aired September 24, 2008:

Announcer: Barack Obama. Born of the corrupt Chicago political machine. Barack Obama: In terms of my toughness. Look, first of all, I come from Chicago. Announcer: His economic advisor, William Daley. Lobbyist, mayor's brother. His money man, Tony Rezko. Client, patron, convicted felon. His political godfather, Emil Jones. Under an ethical cloud. His governor, Rod Blagojevich. A legacy of federal and state investigations. With friends like that, Obama is not ready to lead.
John McCain: I'm John McCain, and I approve this message.
Graphic: Paid for by McCain-Palin 2008. Approved by John McCain.

4. In an e-mail from Bill McInturff, he states, "It [contrast campaign] was to begin on September 15. We did not run the commercial because of the Lehman collapse and instead ran a spot called 'Crisis.' On September 22, we did a press release and released the Chicago ad, but the ad was totally overwhelmed by the environment. Our campaign against Obama was set to begin literally the day the Lehman story hit and then that campaign was gobbled up by events. In a world where the financial collapse did not exist, I believe the campaign, over time, could have been impactful" (e-mail, March 19, 2009).
5. At a Seattle fundraiser on October 19, 2008, Sen. Biden said, "Mark my words, it will not be six months before the world tests Barack Obama like they did John Kennedy. The world is looking. We're about to elect a brilliant 47-year-old senator president of the United States of America. Remember, I said it standing here, if you don't remember anything else I said. Watch, we're going to have an international crisis, a generated crisis, to test the mettle of this guy. He's going to have to make some really tough—I don't know what the decision's going to be, but I promise you it will occur. As a student of history and having served with seven presidents, I guarantee you it's going to happen" (*New York Times* Caucus Blog, October 19, 2008).
6. During a January 9, 2008, visit to speak with Michigan workers, McCain said, "I know how difficult the economy has been here and how tough it's been on the families of this state. And I've got to look you in the eye and say that some of those jobs aren't coming back" (*Detroit Free Press*, January 10, 2008).

Chapter 5
Advertising

Chris Mottola

Chris Mottola *is a nationally recognized political media consultant who most recently worked on Senator John McCain's 2008 campaign for the White House. The commercials Mottola wrote, produced and directed during the 2004 election cycle have won national awards for best internet spot, best congressional commercial, best ballot initiative ad, and best foreign language spot. In addition to his political work, Mottola creates advertising for a number of corporate and public interest concerns. His recent spots advocating stem cell research were considered instrumental in breaking the legislative logjam in Congress. He has lectured before Oxford University (Nuffield College) and the World Affairs Council and is a political contributor to NPR.*

I'm speaking as part of the team that we called Foxhole Productions, which was the media arm of the McCain campaign. The team consisted of myself, Mike Hudome, Fred Davis, and Justin Germany, and, in addition, we had Mark McKinnon kibitzing from the side. We had an ad hoc group with James Farwell and a bunch of other Republican consultants who also gave their advice. Kyle Roberts was the media buyer for the campaign.

I am going to give you an idea from my perspective of what we were trying to do and what we did well and what we did poorly. If you're a media consultant, you're not usually in the room. You're in a small, dark room editing videotape and editing digital 13–14 hours a day. So your perspective at times becomes a little skewed. Of the 100 or so spots that we produced, I'm going to show about nine or ten.

I want to start by saying what a brilliant campaign the Obama people ran. The commentators who said that any Democrat, given the economy, given the environment, could have won this I think are mistaken. I've done six presidential elections. [Their campaign] was about as flawless as you could possibly expect. I think that anybody who sees this as a sheer fact of resources or the economy is really missing the boat. If you want to put this in perspective, since FDR's last race, only one Democrat has gotten a higher percentage of the vote than Barack Obama. If on November 11 a bunch of years back, somebody had said the next president's going to be of mixed race, essentially raised by his grandparents, and his middle name is Hussein, we all would have been doubtful.

The great thing about the McCain campaign was that it threw caution to the wind. Every day was third down and long.

The first spot I want to show was one that Mark McKinnon and Mike Hudome did called "Love for America." You'll see the word "love" throughout the entire thing. In the thematic of the campaign it became country first, love of country. We had a million iterations and a million meetings and a million e-mails. I think this was the key spot of the McCain campaign. It ran in the primary. When you work on a McCain campaign, it's not so much what you poll, it's what he wants to do. This is an almost counterintuitive spot.

TV Advertisement—"Love of America"

JOHN MCCAIN: "Since I've been in Washington I've made a lot of people angry. I made defense contractors angry when I blew the whistle on a 30 billion dollar boondoggle and the culprits were sent to jail. I upset the special interest and Washington lobbyists when I passed campaign finance reform, and made the Pentagon angry when I criticized Rumsfeld's Iraq strategy. I upset the media when I supported the strategy that is now succeeding. I angered the big spenders in Congress when I called for earmark and spending reform. No more 233 million dollar bridges to nowhere or 74 million for peanut storage in a defense spending bill. I didn't go to Washington to win the Mr. Congeniality award. I went to Washington to serve my country. I might not like the business-as-usual crowd in Washington but I love America, I love her enough to make some people angry. I'm John McCain and I approve this message."

GRAPHIC: Paid for by John McCain 2008. Approved by John McCain.

"Love of country" is going to come back as thematic for the campaign. That was the underlying DNA that we always had.

After the primary season's over, we got a bucket of cash. When we were able to spend hard dollars to hard dollars late in the summer and through the convention, we were competitive. We were always a little behind, depending on the survey, but we were in the game.

Chris Mottola

Early on we wanted to frame exactly what we were going to talk about throughout the campaign. This spot was called "6-2-4-7-8-7."

TV Advertisement—"624787"

JOHN MCCAIN: "Keep that faith. Keep your courage. Stick together. Stay strong. Do not yield. Stand up. We're Americans. And we'll never surrender."

ANNOUNCER: What must a president believe about us? About America? That she is worth protecting? That liberty is priceless? Our people, honorable? Our future, prosperous, remarkable and free? And, what must we believe about that president? What does he think? Where has he been? Has he walked the walk?

INTERVIEWER: "What is your rank?"

JOHN MCCAIN: "Lieutenant Commander in the Navy."

INTERVIEWER: "And your official number?"

JOHN MCCAIN: "624787"

ANNOUNCER: John McCain. The American president Americans have been waiting for.

JOHN MCCAIN: "I'm John McCain and I approve this message."

GRAPHIC: Paid for by John McCain 2008. Approved by John McCain.

This ad parallels what we did in what we called the John McCain Poverty Tour, when John McCain went to places that nobody ever went to. We followed it up a week and a half or so later with the service tour.

We wanted to talk about and go to places that no political candidates had gone to since 1960, and no Republican candidate had ever gone to. It was like throwing a stone down a well and hearing the echo.

In the blogosphere, there was this whole thing about our tag line that said "the American President America's been waiting for." Bloggers said, "Oh, they're saying he's a Muslim and he's born in a foreign country." Where that came from was, frankly, totally me. I'm showing my cards here. "We are the ones we've been waiting for?" Instead I said, "The president we've been waiting for." But when Powers Boothe, who was the voiceover, was in the booth, the rhythm was wrong on it. And so I added the "American" president America's been waiting for. That was really the basis for it.

We saw this as a series of essays through which we could frame the election. But it's the old joke about the most elegant battle plans don't survive the first shot. And this was certainly the case.

Number one, they [the tag lines] were very, very hard to write.

We also knew that we had to feed the beast, feed the media every day and give them something to cover and something to talk about. We all got drafted into doing web spots. It was like leaving bright, shiny objects in front of the media to cover the next day or cover in a cycle. Most of them were done by a guy named Justin Germany, who was really the brightest producer on the campaign.

The next spot we called 2013, which is future-based, affirmative. I think more people will have seen it now in this room than actually saw it on the website.

TV Advertisement—"2013"

ANNOUNCER: The year, 2013. The Middle East, stabilized. Nuclear terror threat, reduced. Border security, strengthened. Energy independence, advanced. Wasteful spending, reformed. Health care choice, delivered. Economic confidence, restored. The year, 2013. The president, John McCain.

JOHN MCCAIN: I'm John McCain, and I approve this message.

GRAPHIC: Paid for by John McCain 2008. Approved by John McCain.

The next spot I'm going to show you marked the official kickoff for the campaign. It's called "love." Fred Davis wrote a memo to Mark Weaver in 2007 in which he said that the slogan of the campaign should be "love of country." That's what we were constantly trying to push for in the affirmative. I wrote this 60 [second] bio at a very long meeting with everybody about the difference between McCain and Obama. But frankly, it [was inadequate] because it didn't have a hook to it. And then one night I was going out to dinner, and I had the TV on and saw one of those Time-Life ads, "Hi, I'm David Cassidy. And this is the sounds of the '60s.". . . . I looked it up and found what was called the Summer of Love happened to be the same summer when John McCain was shot down. And so I thought, "Boy, here's a great hook." Because one of our [contrasts] internally—not as text but as subtext, was, "John McCain, public service. Barack Obama, self-service. Self-involvement, [McCain] self-effacement."

And as soon as I figured out it was the "Summer of Love," it was like a dog with a bone. There was push back but I won a battle that one time. This ad was the opening 60 of the general election.

TV Advertisement—"Love 60"

ANNOUNCER: It was a time of uncertainty, hope and change: the summer of love. Half a world away, another kind of love . . . of country. John McCain: shot down, bayoneted, tortured. Offered early release, he said, "No." He'd sworn an oath. Home, he turned to public service. His philosophy: before party, polls and self—America. A maverick, John McCain tackled campaign reform, military reform, spending reform. He took on presidents, partisans and popular opinion. He believes our world is dangerous, our economy in shambles. John McCain doesn't always tell us what we hope to hear. Beautiful words cannot make our lives better. But a man who has always put his country and her people before self, before politics, can. Don't hope for a better life. Vote for one. McCain.

JOHN MCCAIN: I'm John McCain and I approved this message.

GRAPHIC: Paid for by John McCain 2008. Approved by John McCain.

One of the stylistic conceits we used for this, and for all the spots, is a lot of still photos. I think you [the Obama campaign] used a lot more moving photos than we did and moving footage. That creative difference is something that Fred and Mike Hudome and McKinnon and I talked about it a fair amount. The stills made it just a little bit different than your average political spot. Whether the average viewer noticed is debatable. It was very easy to go into the studio and say, "Okay, this is the palette we're working from."

Two things about that spot were the subject of a long discussion. Number one, it would be easy to make the '60s footage at the beginning look like angry '60s footage. I desperately tried to pick stuff that would make you smile. I thought this was lovely footage. What I was trying to say was, "Barack Obama comes out of one part of American politics and John McCain comes out of another." Both are different kinds of love. Let's litigate that out.

The other thing that was a 4:15 in the morning wake-up-in-a-cold-sweat moment was the question, every time that you use John McCain footage of Vietnam, does it make him an old guy? Among my other losing presidential campaigns was Bob Dole's in '96. One of the things I know from that was every time you'd set Bob Dole in World War II, everyone would say, "Is he old." So I was worried about that. But there was evidence that it was not that big a deal because everybody knew he was old.

The next spot was the spot of the campaign. It's a Steve Schmidt spot that was executed by Fred Davis. You've seen it a million times. Think about love, and now think about celebrity, which is the [the name of the] next spot right behind it.

TV Advertisement—"Celebrity"

ANNOUNCER: (NOISE) He's the biggest celebrity in the world. (CROWD CHANTING "OBAMA") But is he ready to lead? With gas prices soaring, Barack Obama says no to offshore drilling? And says he'll raise taxes on electricity? Higher taxes, more foreign oil. That's the real Obama.

JOHN MCCAIN: I'm John McCain and I approve this message.

GRAPHIC: Paid for by John McCain 2008. Approved by John McCain.

The issue content aside, it was really about celebrity. One of the things that the focus groups and the polling said is that there was some initial push back on what I will call the semi-gratuitous use of Paris Hilton. We were saying, "He's important. But what else do we know with him?"

We go to the next one which I call the celebrity tax attack, which is part of the same thematic.

TV Advertisement—"Taxman"

ANNOUNCER: Celebrity? Yes. (CROWD CHANTING "OBAMA") Ready to lead? No. Obama's new taxes could break your family budget. The press warns "the tax man cometh." Obama's taxes mean higher prices at the pump. Obama's taxes, a "recipe for economic disaster." Higher taxes, higher gas prices, economic disaster. That's the real Obama.

JOHN MCCAIN: I'm John McCain and I approve this message.

GRAPHIC: Paid for by John McCain 2008. Approved by John McCain.

It's a filling in the blanks process. . . . Let me go to what I think are strategically and tactically [ads] made of desperation. Because we were being so outspent in hard money, we had to have RNC money [which required that we] do hybrid spots.

The hybrid spots had to be split [in amount of time devoted to McCain and to Republicans] because they were paid for 50/50 with RNC and McCain money. This meant that for every 1,000 points, we got 500 points of McCain messaging. Not to mention the need to split the number of words, which essentially meant incoherent spots.

[Republican consultant] Alex Castellanos e-mailed me and said, "If you have any time left at the end of the spot, you need to say, 'If anyone has any idea what this spot is about, call 1–800-McCain-Palin.'" (LAUGHTER)

This was something that we were kind of desperate about and we were trying to equalize the money. And at a certain point, we realized that in all campaigns, it's about tonnage.

Someone from a radio station asked me, "What's your take on the presidential campaign?" And I said, "Well, like every campaign I've ever been involved with, the person who ran the most negative ads with the most money won." It's flippant and not entirely accurate but to the point.

When you create hybrid ads you have to involve lawyers who say you need to have 30 words for McCain, and 30 for the RNC. You've got to equal those out. So you've got lawyers rewriting spots. Our lawyers were great and they were trying to protect the campaign and John McCain and everybody from liability but the list of great political spots written at 8:00 at night by lawyers with FCC training is zero.

I want to go to our controversial sex education spot. I produced it and thought as I executed it [that] it was probably an overreach. The back end was factually inaccurate and we got our asses kicked in the media. One of the things we were going at wasn't the point that this was a malignant bill or that somehow Barack Obama was insane, but rather "What was he thinking?"

TV Advertisement—"Education"

ANNOUNCER: *Education Week* says Obama hasn't made a significant mark on education. That he's elusive on accountability. A staunch defender of the existing public school monopoly. Obama's one accomplishment? Legislation to teach comprehensive sex education (MUSIC) to kindergarteners. Learning about sex before learning to read? Barack Obama. Wrong on education. Wrong for your family.

JOHN MCCAIN: I'm John McCain and I approve this message.

GRAPHIC: Paid for by McCain-Palin 2008 and the Republican National Committee. Approved by John McCain.

The cultural stuff, the personal stuff, the character stuff, I think, were things that would have happened in a normal campaign. We would have said X, you would have said Y, and we would have debated Z. . . . I'm going to play two in a row, the Bill Ayers spot and the Chicago spot. Early in September, we had this 6-week economic meltdown. When I picked up my paper every day, it wasn't about McCain, it wasn't about Palin, it was about how bad does the Republican economy suck today. If you thought Bill Ayers was a bad guy, or if you thought Barack Obama was a bad guy, it didn't matter because we can politically vivisect these people afterward but I just lost 20 percent of my retirement.

These ads are also those awful hybrids. By the way, we were still doing still photos.

TV Advertisement—"Ambition"

ANNOUNCER: Obama's blind ambition. When convenient, he worked with terrorist, Bill Ayers. When discovered, he lied. Blind ambition, bad judgment. Congressional liberals fought for risky subprime loans. Congressional liberals fought against more regulation. Then the housing market collapsed costing you billions. In crisis, we need leadership, not bad judgment.

JOHN MCCAIN: I'm John McCain and I approve this message.

GRAPHIC: Paid for by McCain-Palin 2008 and the Republican National Committee. Approved by John McCain.

The economy drowned all this out. Didn't matter.

TV Advertisement—"Unethical"

ANNOUNCER: Obama rewards his friends with your tax dollars. Tony Rezko $14 million, Allison Davis, $20 million, Kenny Smith, $100,000. Congressional liberals promised to raise your taxes. To reward their friends with wasteful pork. Taxes for you, pork for them, who's gonna stop 'em? Congressional liberals? Or him?

JOHN MCCAIN: I'm John McCain and I approve this message.

GRAPHIC: Paid for by McCain-Palin 2008 and the Republican National Committee. Approved by John McCain.

We finally got to the end of the hybrid spots and back to where we needed to be. The next spot is a comparison spot that Fred Davis did after he and I kicked it back and forth forever. It said: He's for this, I'm for that in simple, plain language.

TV Advertisement—"Your Choice"

ANNOUNCER: Your choice. For higher taxes. For workin' Joe's. Spread your income. Keep what's yours. A trillion in new spending. Free spending. Eliminate waste. Paying for small business. Economic growth. Risky. Proven. For a stronger America, McCain.

JOHN MCCAIN: I'm John McCain, and I approve this message.

GRAPHIC: Paid for by the Republican National Committee and authorized by McCain-Palin 2008. Approved by John McCain.

Coming out of the convention, we had a lead or were tied, depending on who you listened to. We then got overwhelmed and finally picked up the bar late in the campaign. But I think that the hybrid stuff combined in that 4- or 6-week period [with the economic meltdown and the Obama financial advantage] was just devastating to us.

It was not like we had other options open to us. The question we faced was "Do you want the arsenic or the cyanide?" The last three spots I will show illustrate that we were trying to raise the stakes again. The first is a spot that Fred Davis did about foreign policy called "Tiny" ["Iran"]. By this point, foreign policy had shrunk in importance in the polls. At the same time, Iraq reappeared briefly in the news, so we threw it on the air.

My favorite person in all this thing is not Joe the plumber, but Joe Biden. You know, at the end of the campaign, Joe Biden was the only person we really had doing credible negative on Obama. And so, I'll play that and the last spot which is essentially a summation of the campaign which is how we ended up.

TV Advertisement—"Iran"

ANNOUNCER: Iran. Radical Islamic government. Known sponsors of terrorism. Developing nuclear capabilities to generate power. But threatening to eliminate Israel. Obama says Iran is a tiny country. It doesn't pose a serious threat. Terrorism? Destroying Israel? Those aren't serious threats? Obama, dangerously unprepared to be president.

JOHN MCCAIN: I'm John McCain, and I approve this message.

GRAPHIC: Paid for by John McCain 2008. Approved by John McCain.

TV Advertisement—"Listen to Biden"

ANNOUNCER: Listen to Joe Biden talking about what electing Barack Obama will mean.

JOE BIDEN: Mark my words. It will not be six months before the world tests Barack Obama. The world's looking. We're going to have an international crisis to test the mettle of this guy. I guarantee you it's gonna happen.

ANNOUNCER: It doesn't have to happen. Vote McCain.

JOHN MCCAIN: I'm John McCain, and I approve this message.

GRAPHIC: Paid for by John McCain 2008. Approved by John McCain.

TV Advertisement—"Special"

ANNOUNCER: Behind the fancy speeches, promises, and TV specials lies the truth. With crises at home and abroad, Barack Obama lacks the experience America needs, and it shows. His response to our economic crisis is to spend and tax our economy deeper into recession. The fact is, Barack Obama's not ready yet.

JOHN MCCAIN: I'm John McCain, and I approve this message.

GRAPHIC: Paid for by McCain-Palin 2008. Approved by John McCain.

We had a horrible hand to play in the general election. You've all been in campaigns where when the ship goes bad, it goes sideways really quickly. There's entropy to the whole thing.

But the bottom line is, Republicans were the party in power. And the Democratic question was, "do you want more of the same?" And we had to say "Well, there's a guy you like, we—you don't really know a lot about him. So, here's some information you might know about him which may or may not be really convincing. So what do you think?"

Whenever we'd get a grab a little toehold in a state, you [the Obama campaign] would dump [something] like 5,000 points in Wilkes-Barre/Scranton and explode the whole thing out for us.

Jim Margolis

Jim Margolis, a senior partner at GMMB, has worked for years at the intersection of politics, advertising, and advocacy on behalf of candidates, foundations, government agencies, and corporate clients. In presidential politics, Margolis served as a senior advisor to Barack Obama in his campaign for the White House, leading advertising efforts for Mr. Obama as part of the core strategic team. GMMB also served as the lead agency for Bill Clinton's first presidential race. Overseas, Margolis has helped direct presidential and prime ministerial contests in Latin America, Africa, Central America and Asia. He has been recognized nationally and internationally for his work.

In the advertising from the beginning to the end we settled on a few strategic imperatives that were in synch with who Barack Obama was and where he came from. The first imperative was that we needed to own change. Second, we had to focus relentlessly on the economy which we did throughout. Third, there was a dimension that was about reassurance. We needed to send the right cultural cues indicating that we were totally right on a lot of those values issues.

Experience was not an area that we spent a large amount of time worrying about either in the primary or in the general election. We really felt, as David [Axelrod] pointed out earlier, that by the end of the campaign, after the debates and seeing him throughout this process, people would conclude that he was prepared to be president of the United States.

We also were determined to expand the map. That was something that was at the core of who we were and what we were going to do in the field and in advertising as well.

Second, we were determined to expand the electorate. We were looking for new voters and using advertising to appeal to specific groups.

Third, we saw in our testing that our greatest competitive advantage was our guy. Everybody's talked about it today. There would be ads that we thought were great, creative ads. We'd test them and every time [the ad featuring] Barack Obama would rise to the top. He was that good.

He knew why he wanted to be president. The consistency that we had in our message, from the slogan to what we showed in our advertising [and] from the first advertisement to our last, was fundamentally about change.

The money situation allowed us to keep a positive track up throughout the entire campaign. And even while we were clobbering Senator McCain, we had the ability to still have something out there every single day that was telling people why you should elect this guy and why you should feel confident about him being president of the United States.

This chart shows spending on primary advertising. Overall, there was about $96 million spent on pro-Obama advertising with just a fraction coming from Independent Expenditures like SEIU and others.

Hillary Clinton lands at about $51 million after which the rest becomes pretty insignificant. That was the primary.

This shows our spending versus Hillary Clinton's over the course of the campaign. After Super Tuesday, we had the capacity to dominate until the very end when we both spent about the same amount.

In the general, we will end up at about $314 million in spending on the media side with a little bit from outside groups with the McCain campaign ending up at about $146, $147 million.

For a lot of the early [general election] period there weren't huge differences in spending. There were a couple weeks in which [the Republicans] actually were bumping up ahead of us a little bit at least by our calculation. In the September period we began to have the capacity to advertise on multiple tracks.

By way of comparison, in some of these battleground states, we were able to be at 14 million, compared to McCain in Colorado, 13. That was pretty much a toss-up with the RNC combination. Nevada, 8 versus 5.

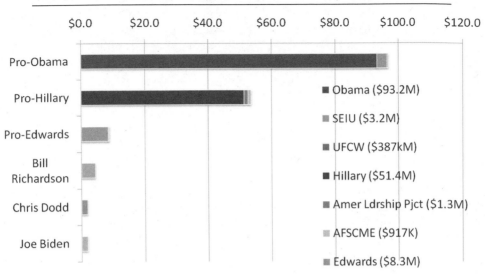

CHART 16. PRIMARY ELECTION SPENDING (IN MILLIONS)

Legend:
- Obama ($93.2M)
- SEIU ($3.2M)
- UFCW ($387kM)
- Hillary ($51.4M)
- Amer Ldrship Pjct ($1.3M)
- AFSCME ($917K)
- Edwards ($8.3M)

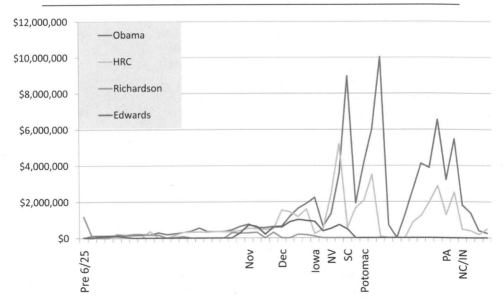

CHART 17. PRIMARY TV SPENDING (IN MILLIONS)

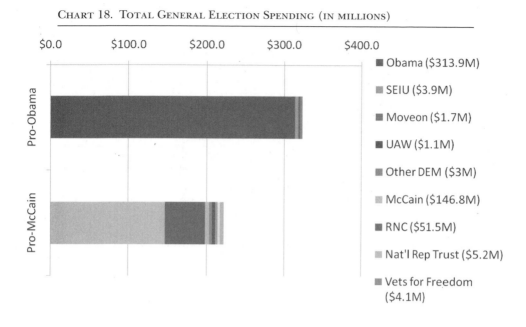

CHART 18. TOTAL GENERAL ELECTION SPENDING (IN MILLIONS)

- Obama ($313.9M)
- SEIU ($3.9M)
- Moveon ($1.7M)
- UAW ($1.1M)
- Other DEM ($3M)
- McCain ($146.8M)
- RNC ($51.5M)
- Nat'l Rep Trust ($5.2M)
- Vets for Freedom ($4.1M)

CHART 19. GENERAL CANDIDATE TV SPENDING CALENDAR

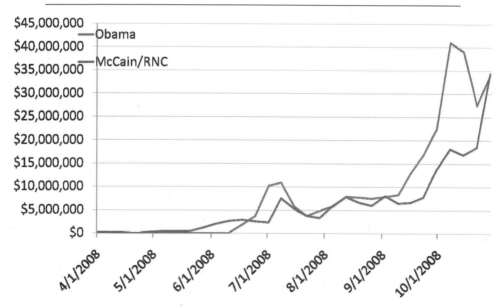

CHART 20. BATTLEGROUND TV SPENDING COMPARISON IN THE GENERAL
ELECTION

	Obama	McCain
Colorado	$14.4	$13.9
Florida	$36.1	$16.2
Ohio	$31.5	$30.6
North Carolina	$15.6	$ 5.6
Pennsylvania	$31.4	$25.0
Nevada	$ 8.7	$ 5.5
Virginia	$26.0	$14.0
Indiana	$13.3	$ 5.3
*Dollar amounts in millions		

CHART 21. OBAMA FOR AMERICA SPOT NUMBERS

	Primary Election	General Election
Aired Spots	95	100
Produced Spots	148	253

Virginia, 26 versus 14. Florida, 36 versus 16. North Carolina, 15 versus 5. Indiana, 13 versus 5.

Pennsylvania, 31 versus 25. And Ohio, 31/30. We were pretty at parity there. But in a lot of these states, we had some capacity to play. Next slide, please. This is sad, right here, to Chris's point about being in tiny little studios late—late at night.

We produced over 400 ads in the primary and the general election, of which we aired about 200. There were many variations on a theme and different versions. But these were unique spots that might change a little bit. And we aren't counting those changes.

We did a huge amount of testing, both attack and response, of what we thought you would come at us with.

Here are the tracks. We ran general market media—that was general advertising, national and spot. These weren't taking place everywhere across the country: Women's track, often a senior track, often a youth track. We had some rural media, both TV and radio. More radio. An African American track. A Hispanic track. And then a "big events" track. Olympics, Super Bowl, and World Series. And then the long-form media. We had the ability to air sixties, two-minute spots, and the thirty

Jim Margolis

minute program. We are saying, "This is not an infomercial, it's a pilot."
And we had Obama On Demand which we negotiated with Dish Network and DirecTV.

Forty-five million people went to On Demand, in one form or
another, [and] stayed an average of 12 minutes each, to pick the pro-
gramming they wanted to see. It was an important thing for us.

The 30-minute show was watched by 35 million people—across the
country and that doesn't count web exposure. There were three essential pillars that we communicated throughout the course of this campaign. The first was the unity pillar. We need a president who's going to
unite us, not divide us, a president who will restore a sense of common
purpose. Second, we need a president who will change the ways of Washington and who will focus on middle-class concerns. More of the same
just won't do. That was a consistent message in the primary season and
in the general. Third, we need a president who will be honest with you,
who will talk straight to you. This was an honesty pillar. And overall,
through all of this advertising, we tried to express optimism—the "wil-

l.i.am" incarnation of our "Yes, We Can," message. There was something hopeful and uplifting about this candidacy.

This spot, taken from the Jefferson Jackson Day dinner, early in Iowa, and was then taken across the country was, I think, a pretty good encapsulation of these messages.

TV Advertisement—"Our Moment Is Now"

BARACK OBAMA: We are in a defining moment in our history. Our nation is at war. The planet is in peril. The dream that so many generations fought for feels as if it's slowly slipping away. And that is why the same old Washington textbook campaigns just won't do. That's why telling the American people what we think they want to hear, instead of telling the American people what they need to hear just won't do. (CHEERING). America, our moment is now. I don't want to spend the next year or the next four years re-fighting the same fights that we had in the 1990s. I don't want to pit red America against blue America. I want to be the President of the United States of America! (CHEERING)

GRAPHIC: Approved by Barack Obama. Paid for by Obama for America.

So that started in Iowa. What you saw was a Texas version of the spot. To your question earlier about African American audiences, this spot was shown in South Carolina. At first, I was worried that we didn't have enough African American faces to go there. It turned out, as we did the research and the focus group work, that it was critical that people saw the white faces. For those [African American] audiences to recognize that this was somebody who had been embraced [by whites] and got that kind of a response in Iowa was meaningful to them saying, "Okay, I'm ready to take the plunge and believe that this can actually happen."

The next spot played heavily in the primary in many different states. It is called "Enough" and was pretty consistently a good performer.

TV Advertisement—"Enough"

BARACK OBAMA: I'm Barack Obama, and I approve this message. Ordinary people all across the country are struggling from paycheck to paycheck. If the plant moves to China and you've been working there for 20, 30 years and suddenly you have the rug pulled out from under you, and you don't have health care and you don't have a pension, you're on your own. We've got to stop giving tax breaks to companies that are moving overseas and give those tax breaks to companies that are investing in the United States of America. (APPLAUSE). Enough is enough.

GRAPHIC: Approved by Barack Obama. Paid for by Obama for America.

One of the other things that we always tried to do is have spots that went to values somewhere in the mix. This education spot ran in a number of different states during the primaries. It came back in the general because it worked very well. It aligned him on the values set of issues like personal responsibility. The key line in this spot says that "government can't do it all. Parents need to turn off the TV, take responsibility for their kids." Coming from Barack Obama that was an important signal that we needed to send to people.

TV Advertisement—"Education Plan, Oregon"

BARACK OBAMA: For me, the American Dream began in a room like this. My family didn't have much money. But education made everything possible. I'm Barack Obama and want kids all across Oregon to have that chance. As President, I'll expand early childhood education, recruit new teachers, and pay them better. But the truth is, government can't do it all. As parents, we need to turn off the TV, read to our kids, give them that thirst to learn. I approve this message because it's not just about their future, it's about ours.

GRAPHIC: Approved by Barack Obama. Paid for by Obama for America.

As we got to places like Pennsylvania, and I'd argue Ohio and Texas, too, there were moments when I think we got into a back and forth with Senator Clinton and became a little snarky and a little small. We talked a lot about the snark factor. I think that is where we did not serve Senator Obama as well we should have. We were tonally off a little bit. The gas tax holiday spot that you're about to see was an example of one of those moments when we captured him. He looked courageous. We were in a good spot. And we were back tonally where we needed to be. This spot ran in Indiana and North Carolina.

TV Advertisement—"Truth"

BARACK OBAMA: I'm Barack Obama, and I approve this message. So, I'm here to tell you the truth. We could suspend the gas tax for six months. But that's not going to bring down gas prices long-term. You're going to save about $25, $30. (LAUGHTER). Or half a tank a gas. (LAUGHTER). That's typical of how Washington works. There's a problem. Everybody's upset about gas prices. Let's find some short-term, quick fix that we can say we did something even though we're not really doing anything. We cannot deliver on a better energy policy unless we change how business is done in Washington. We've got to go out to the oil companies and look at their price-gouging, and we've got to start using less oil. And that means raising fuel efficiency standards on cars and developing alternative fuels. That's the real, honest answer to how we're going to solve this problem. That's what you need from a president, somebody who's going to tell you the truth.

GRAPHIC: Approved by Barack Obama. Paid for by Obama for America.

Pillars: honesty and reform.

As noted earlier we had multiple tracks. I wanted to show you an example of one of the youth spots that ran just on youth media from WB to MTV. Notice the text messaging. Everything was connected back up to engage people and bring them into the process.

TV Advertisement—"We Can"

BARACK OBAMA: We want an end to this war. And we want diplomacy and peace. Not only can we save the environment, we can create jobs and—and opportunity. We're tired of fear, we're tired of division. We want something new. We want to turn the page. (CHEERING). The world as it is, is not the world as it has to be.

GRAPHIC: BarackObama.com/change. Paid for by Obama for America.

Moving to the general election. Let me first say, we had a great team. Originally, in the primaries, AKP&D, David's firm, and GMMB did virtually all the work. We expanded the team in the general election when we needed more help. Let me just say, people worked tremendously well together.

So Murphy Putnam and Dixon Davis and Saul Shorr from here in Philadelphia, and Squier Knapp Dunn and James Aldrete and SSK, and

Fuse and Larry Grisolano, who helped coordinate and put all these pieces together, were really important. Everyone worked as one unit.

In the general election we continued the positive positioning that we had set up in the primary. We felt that we needed to keep filling in [Senator Obama's] biography, which we did in the beginning of the summer.

This 60-second spot actually ran a little bit later, but is indicative of the longer form track. We wanted to reinforce values.

TV Advertisement—"Grandfather"

BARACK OBAMA: I'm Barack Obama, and I approve this message. One of my earliest memories, going with my grandfather to see some of the astronauts being brought back after a splashdown, sitting on his shoulders, and waving a little American flag. And—and my grandfather, you know, would say, "Boy, Americans, we can do anything, well, when we put our minds to it."

ANNOUNCER: His grandfather fought in Patton's army. His grandmother worked on a bomber assembly line. But it was his mother who would see in him a promise.

BARACK OBAMA: My mother, she said to herself, you know, "My son, he's an American and he needs to understand what that means." She'd wake me up at 4:30 in the morning and we'd sit there and go through my lessons. And I used to complain and grumble. And she'd say, "Well, this is no picnic for me either, buster."

ANNOUNCER: His life was shaped by the values he learned as a boy.

BARACK OBAMA: Hard work. Honesty. Self-reliance. Respect for other people. Kindness. Faith. That's the country I believe in.

GRAPHIC: Approved by Barack Obama. Paid for by Obama for America.

Putting his arms around the lady in the ad. People like to talk about that. David [Axelrod] earlier talked about how people look at presidential elections. As he said, our premise was that voters didn't want a replica; they wanted a remedy. That was the premise upon which our general election campaign was built.

We carried that through. McCain represented a Bush third term; he was more of the same. His 26 years in Washington didn't make a case for change. We prosecuted that idea throughout the campaign.

Every ad we produced in some way went to that thematic. Whether it was the economy or Iraq or choice, [we argued] that Senator McCain embraced those same policies as Bush. He couldn't be change, if he was embracing those policies. In effect, Barack was the antidote to the Bush attributes.

The next ad tried to put together "fundamentals of the economy" and "out of touch" in one spot.

TV Advertisement—"Seven"

BARACK OBAMA: I'm Barack Obama, and I approve this message.

ANNOUNCER: Maybe you're struggling just to pay the mortgage on your home. But recently, John McCain said, the fundamentals of our economy are strong. Hum. Then again, that same day when asked how many houses he owns? McCain lost track. He couldn't remember. Well, it's seven. Seven houses. And here's one house America can't afford to let John McCain move into.

GRAPHIC: Approved by Barack Obama. Paid for by Obama for America.

And another example has a more humorous twist to it. Saul Shorr had written the script. I loved the concept. And eventually, we got it on the air in the summer.

TV Advertisement—"Don't Know Much"

BARACK OBAMA: I'm Barack Obama, and I approve this message.

SINGING: I'm not up on the economy. Don't know much about industry. Really can't explain the price of gas. Or what has happened to the middle class. But I know that one and one is two. And if I could be just like you, what a wonderful world this would be.

ANNOUNCER: Do we really want four more years of the same old tune?

GRAPHIC: Approved by Barack Obama. Paid for by Obama for America.

The [notion that] we can't afford more of the same was really the hook for the general election. Middle class tax cuts were the affirmative case. I don't have those for you today. But we also hit the negative side.

For us to have been able to neutralize the tax issue was an important thing to accomplish. Two ads:

TV Advertisement—"Unravel"

BARACK OBAMA: I'm Barack Obama, and I approve this message.

ANNOUNCER: It could all unravel. Your health care under John McCain. McCain would tax health benefits for the first time ever, meaning higher income taxes for millions. His plan would raise costs for employers offering health care. So your coverage could be reduced or even dropped completely. And since McCain won't require coverage for pre-existing conditions, finding a new plan could leave you hanging by a thread. It's not the change we need.

GRAPHIC: Approved by Barack Obama. Paid for by Obama for America.

TV Advertisement—"Tax Health Care"

ANNOUNCER: John McCain talks about a $5,000 tax credit for health care. But here's what he's not telling you. McCain would make you pay income tax on your health insurance benefits, taxing health benefits for the first time ever. And that tax credit? McCain's own website says it goes straight to the insurance companies, not to you. Leaving you on your own to pay McCain's health insurance tax. Taxing health care instead of fixing it. We can't afford John McCain.

BARACK OBAMA: I'm Barack Obama, and I approve this message.

GRAPHIC: Approved by Barack Obama. Paid for by Obama for America.

Toward the end of the campaign when the Republicans were beginning to distance a bit from the president, we got to the [October 15] debate. All of us were doing post-debate spots. Unfortunately, you used to finish them a lot earlier than we did. I don't know why it took us so long. The McCain team would be out in like 15 minutes. You must have produced them the day before.

We saw the moment that was going to be the sound bite for the spot. Senator McCain was distancing from the president. We decided to go straight at it, to try to use jujitsu here. Embrace it and turn it around. This is "90 percent."

TV Advertisement—"90 Percent"

BARACK OBAMA: I'm Barack Obama, and I approve this message.

JOHN MCCAIN: Senator Obama, I am not President Bush.

ANNOUNCER: True, but you did vote with Bush 90 percent of the time. Tax breaks for big corporations and the wealthy, but almost nothing for the middle class. Same as Bush. Keep spending $10 billion a month in Iraq while our own economy struggles? Same as Bush. You may not be George Bush but—

JOHN MCCAIN: I voted with the President over 90 percent of the time, higher than—a lot of my—even Republican colleagues.

GRAPHIC: Approved by Barack Obama. Paid for by Obama for America.

We used that clip quite a bit. This was an example of a press ad.

I thought [the McCain campaign] were masterful in using the press. It started in September, or late August. It happened throughout. Both campaigns were staying up all night producing a spot to be at the stations at 6:00 a.m. the next morning. It went from something that we would all periodically do to a daily thing.

David Plouffe said [to reporters], "Are you guys crazy? These aren't really running." It's running one time in Harrisburg, and you are running it on a loop on CNN as if it's real.

Finally, this was one of the positive spots at the end, trying to get back to values and what he stands for, trying to reassure that he was a safe choice.

TV Advertisement—"What I Believe"

BARACK OBAMA: John McCain wants to scare you. I want you to know what I believe. I believe in the dignity of work. I believe in tax cuts for the middle class. I believe people who break the law should be punished. And the terrorists who plot against us should be hunted down before they strike. I believe we need to fund our schools. But that no money can take the place of a parent taking responsibility for their child. And I believe in you and our ability to make America even better. I'm Barack Obama and I approve this message.

GRAPHIC: Approved by Barack Obama. Paid for by Obama for America.

MARK WALLACE:

Did you ever have a moment where you were having a hard time buying ads because there's not enough available air time? Or did you ever turn on the TV in a market and say, "Oh, my God, look at all our ads?"

JIM MARGOLIS:

Clearly, we had a lot of fire power operating in these key markets. There were moments when we talked about whether we had reached saturation. In fact, there were a couple of moments where we actually pulled back in some areas.

We also made decisions not to go into some areas where we were already at very, very high levels. This is one reason that we liked the different tracks. We didn't feel that people were getting tired if they were seeing a two-minute spot of him direct to camera followed by a 30-second that would hit [McCain].

BILL MCINTURFF:

Candidates talk for two years; they make mistakes. There's a record. All that's pretty fair. But there is a [troubling] Spanish language ad called, "John McCain's Friends."[1] John McCain imploded his primary trying to pass conference of immigration reform. And in your ad, Rush Limbaugh's on the air calling them [Latinos] stupid and lazy. And [the suggestion in the ad is that] he is John McCain's friend.

What's your own thought about this spot about John [McCain] not being able to use a Blackberry,[2] given that he can't use his hands, or using Rush in a spot on immigration reform?

JIM MARGOLIS:

[On the computer ad,] David has said probably in retrospect, if we had to do it over again, we wouldn't do it. We read clips where he had said he had been trying to learn the computer and e-mailing. So, we did not feel, given that we had read that beforehand, that this was something that was physically impossible for him to do. We would not have done the ad if we had understood that to be the case. We would not have run that spot.

DAVID AXELROD:

On immigration, I think it's fair to say that with the volume of stuff that we were doing that quality control occasionally became an issue. I'd say that. And very rarely. I think we were pretty assiduous.

JIM MARGOLIS:

That's what I was going to say. 400 spots. I don't think there were more than two or three.

DAVID AXELROD:

And I would say on the [computer-use] spot [that] that was an example of what I was talking about. That was a press spot. It was purely driven by filling a hole to try and drive some cable.

On the Rush [Limbaugh] piece, I think there was fair push back on it. I will say this. I don't want to start a big debate here because I do respect Senator McCain for what he's done on this issue but there was this sort of back and forth in the Republican debate.

ANITA DUNN:

I'm a little exercised because I think if we want to start going down the road of ads that were put on, particularly the press ads that were produced, Bill, we can raise questions about why Franklin Raines [Raines is black], somebody who had been identified in one article as having advised Senator Obama once, was picked to be the face of Fannie Mae and Freddie Mac, as opposed to Jim Johnson, who'd been the initial head of our VP [vetting team]. I would think there are all kinds of press ads that we could discuss at that point.

DAVID AXELROD:

Barack Obama had met Franklin Raines once at a social event for five minutes. So, there's no doubt that if you get down to fact-check world we've all got scars to bear here.

CHRIS MOTTOLA:

David, I want to defend you on this. One of the things in this process is that you are tired.

The candidates are tired; everybody's tired, and stuff that you would normally not do on a 40-hour work week slips [through]. The big joke was "What do you call a 40-hour work week?" "Tuesday night."

ANITA DUNN:

I think that both campaigns, when we made those mistakes, and when we got to those lines, it was because of the necessity of providing content for the press.

BROOKS JACKSON, FACTCHECK.ORG:

Just wanted to ask about these press ads. Do you feel that you have to run them at all? Before you hand it to Wolf Blitzer, do you feel that it actually has to have one paid run or is this just purely for a hand-out?

JIM MARGOLIS:

Well, it doesn't have to [actually air] for Wolf to run it. But most of the time, we'd put it up.

CHRIS MOTTOLA:

We say "we're putting this on the air. We're going to put this on the air. We may put this on the air." It doesn't matter.

BROOKS JACKSON:

Just a comment. I fought this at CNN when we fact-checked an ad. Let's wait and see if it's running or not.

JIM MARGOLIS:

It doesn't matter, Brooks. Even when we demonstrated that the ad wasn't running, they would run the story.

DAVID AXELROD:

The *New York Times* did a full piece on it and—it ran once in Pittsburgh or something. And we told them that.

JIM MARGOLIS:

Yeah.

DAVID AXELROD:

It was a way into the story. And that's of course why you did it.

CHRIS MOTTOLA:

We need to produce web spots like I need another hole in my head.

JOEL BENENSON:

In this YouTube world, when Hillary ran the 3:00 a.m. ad in Texas, and they released it on Friday morning, our Sunday night tracker in Ohio reported that 54 percent of the voters there had seen the ad, which is astonishing over a two-day period without it ever airing in their state.

Notes

1. "Immigration" aired in mid-September:

Barack Obama: "I'm Barack Obama and I approve this message."
[Announcer, Translated from Spanish]: Even when they insult us they want us to tolerate it. [Text on Screen]: ". . . Mexicans are stupid and not quali-fied."—Rush Limbaugh. [Announcer]: Intolerance—they tell us it's imag-ined in this country that so many of us love. [Text on Screen]: "Shut your mouth or get out!"—Rush Limbaugh. [Announcer]: John McCain and his Republican friends have two faces: They tell us lies to get our votes and the other, worse still, he follows the failed policies of George Bush. He puts the interests of powerful groups above the interests of families and workers. John McCain—more of the same Republican tricks."
Graphic: Obama for America/Democratic National Committee.

2. See Chapter 2, note 1.

Chapter 6

The Campaign and the Press

Nicolle Wallace

The notion that John McCain changed vis-à-vis the media should be corrected. The media had that backward. John McCain was sad that the media had changed so drastically from 2000. He missed the media from 2000. The media in 2000 were a press corps that got on a bus and spent a day talking about an issue. They would usually have to say to him, "Senator McCain, we'd love to keep talking to you, but we've got to file." They'd take the benefit of all that conversation and file.

The media of 2008 would get on a bus leg in the middle of a conversation, type out a blog about how his sock was down or didn't match his shoe. He was sad that their industry had put these pressures on them, that they could no longer have discussions about issues that took place over the course of the day, as you rolled around on the bus for eight hours.

I think he also missed the media of 2000 because in 2000 they had access to him on the bus but they also included images or sounds or other things that they saw on a campaign trail. By 2008, the only thing that made air were questions about Viagra—the gotcha moment. I think he remained quite distraught for what had happened to journalism.

It did change a lot between 2000 and 2008. Howard Kurtz (of CNN and the *Washington Post*) came out with us and said, "You know, all these guys back here, some of them were 12 [years old] in 2000. So, they don't even know what they're talking about. And they say they miss the John McCain of 2000." He asked, "What does Senator McCain think?" I said, "He just chuckles and says he misses the press corps of the year 2000 and of the 2000 campaign." I think the media can't help itself when they're part of a story. The coverage of the relationship between John McCain and the media was always about the media.

We paid a big price for his commitment to accessibility. John McCain can't and won't be handled. It's not as if campaign staff would say, "No more media." He'd laugh at you and say, "Get out of Elisabeth Bumill-

Nicolle Wallace and Anita Dunn

er's [*New York Times* reporter] seat." It's not as if anyone said to him, "Enough." He finally saw an inability to communicate a message over the course of the summer which, once the Democratic primary ended, really mattered. Since we didn't have resources, we relied on those news cycles. It's why the "show me" ads, as we called them, were part of our strategy. We didn't have curtain number two, three or four. We really relied on our media. We just couldn't spare any more news cycles to insipid conversations about Viagra. So, we made a decision to change our interactions. We moved them out of the back of the bus. We started using that for speech writing and working. It became a traveling office instead of a rolling press conference. We really tried to change our approach to message.

Another thought, I don't know how many of you have ever come home with a new puppy. How many people have ever come home with a puppy? Raised a puppy? I had a very smart, willful, stubborn puppy. I'd say, "Why is she jumping?" She'd bark right at my face. The trainer said, "She has impulse control problems. You need to train her to resist the impulse." And I said, "How do I do that?" We had a whole bag of hot dogs that we'd carry around. You literally train an animal out of the impulse to express every urge.

The media has an impulse control problem. It cannot help itself. It cannot help itself from jumping on the seediest or the most unseemly or the most unsubstantiated rumor. Then all the reporters who have plenty of impulse control, who are working real stories or looking at issues feel all these puppies breathing down their neck, because they're chasing the hot dogs.

What we ended up with in the big cauldron of political coverage was really a lot a crap. Some did a good job. But the changes in journalism made it harder for someone like Dan Balz or Adam Nagourney or Elisabeth Bumiller to spend the day working her contacts, making calls, talking with campaigns and writing a story. Because every 30 minutes, she's on her Blackberry and someone's filed about how, at the last event—someone threw a naked Palin Barbie. And someone has to file that. There was so much junk in that system. It leaves a lot of questions for journalists and journalism to examine. When something bad happens at a government agency, sometimes the best way to investigate it is a self-audit. It's probably a moment in political coverage for political journalism inside some of the best journalism schools to look inside and ask what they want to be. Because to turn the really good political journalists into people who have to compete with—

ANITA DUNN:

With the political—

NICOLLE WALLACE:

—the bloggers all day is a different deal. It's a different beat. Steve and I used to say, we ran the last campaign of the last century of campaigns in media acts. It will be viewed as quaint that we rolled around on a bus with a pool.

I was at the White House for six years. And one of the things we started grappling with was what's a journalist? People who wrote online articles for websites hosted by companies say, we're in-house journalists. What is a journalist? And what's their obligation vis-à-vis political coverage?

I know that NBC internally grappled with the presence of Keith Olbermann on its brand. We had a lot of meetings at the highest levels of NBC. I think Brian Williams is a very, very committed journalist. But

Keith Olbermann said some of the ugliest, nastiest things, things that I wouldn't repeat in mixed company about Cindy McCain, about the Palin kids. I mean, forget about the politicians. They sign up for it. But when you've got both candidates ruling spouses and kids off bounds, and you've got Keith Olbermann saying really nasty things, it makes the relationship with the news side of the network hard. All we ever said was, "It's a difficult thing for us. It's difficult for us to sit here or to pull back the curtain and share with you when on the way to the bathroom, we could run into Keith Olbermann."

I know NBC grapples with it. They have made business decisions that are what they are. I joined the campaign in April of '08, and I said, "You better hope and pray that we lose, because we are on such a bad path that—don't know what would happen if Senator McCain had won and had to continue to deal with MSNBC and NBC."

I think by the end, it was in a more positive place, largely through the efforts of Tom Brokaw, Brian Williams, and people like Chuck Todd, people who took very seriously our concerns about the MSNBC, NBC family. . . .

When you're in communications, you're drinking out of the fire hose. You've got all the news created by your own campaign to deal with, the ads, the ads that come from the other side. You've got the changing and evolving relationship with the political press. And then you're always on the front line of whatever is coming your way from, in our case, a very organized, very strategic, very methodical opponent.

It was certainly not a campaign without challenges and I worked for a candidate who really gets the media and really valued the relationships that he had. What I came away with is that there are still places in journalism where source reporting, where those relationships really matter.

I believe that it's worth examining whether in this election newspapers, your local dailies and to a slightly lesser extent, the national papers and network television coverage and local television coverage, reemerged as arbiters of the information that got through to the most number of voters. There were certainly things that were spread on the Internet. But they were largely seen by groups of voters that were very much interested and in favor of one candidate or the other. . . . I think news outlets and television networks can now become something different and just as useful, and perhaps even more valuable. And that is organizers and prioritizers of information.

Anita Dunn

Anita Dunn, *most recently senior advisor and chief communications officer to the successful campaign of President-Elect Barack Obama, has been a top political* *strategist and communications advisor for nearly three decades. In 2001–2002, Dunn served as senior political advisor to Senate Democratic Leader Tom Daschle as well as consultant to the Senate Democratic Caucus when they gained the majority. In the House of Representatives, Dunn has advised Speaker of the House Nancy Pelosi. She has also served as chief strategist and media consultant to senior Democratic Members facing challenging reelection battles. Dunn joined the firm of Squier Knapp Dunn in 1993.*

I joined the Obama campaign in January of 2008 and I was a friend of the Obama campaign throughout 2007. I had not worked on the 2004 presidential campaign. When I came on a regular basis in January of 2008, right after New Hampshire, one of the first things that everyone said to me was, "You will be astonished when you go out on the bus the first time, and you see how young everybody is." Astonished wasn't even the word. I thought, "Geez, I thought everybody on the campaign was so young." The time I walked into the campaign, I'd never felt older in my life. You can only imagine what the Obama campaign was like.

I think what Nicolle has just said is extraordinarily important, which is that the nature of campaign coverage in 2008 was totally reactive. It was non-stop. There was no context and no analysis. I was shocked for at least two days, until we figured out exactly how we wanted to play it.

We were in the primaries up against one of the more famous political machines of the last century, the Clintons, the legendary war room people. They had an aggressive press operation. What was interesting to me was the ability that our campaign developed with the help of Jon [Carson] and—and Joe Rospers and the people in New Media, to communicate around the filter. You need to feed cable and the Internet with content. We would occasionally say [cynically], "They need new bright, shiny things to go play with," which would be that [web] advertising we forced [the ad team] to produce. We tried to resist that and keep our campaign integrity for a while but at the end of the day, there was a national narrative that cable and the Internet were telling. There was a campaign they were talking about that was actually not the real campaign. That was, to me, one of the most interesting things I've ever seen.

Those of us who are old grew up in an era in which you were taught that your earned media, your press, should support what your paid media were doing. In this world, what you were doing in the press was supposed to reinforce what you were doing in the paid media. Your speeches, your surrogates, and everybody were supposed to be saying the same thing.

What you've increasingly got in 2008, at least from our campaign, was

Anita Dunn

what I call the total disconnect. You had this bizarre national narrative, this weird 24-hour national campaign that was being played out on cable and on blogs and on Internet sites.

NICOLLE WALLACE:

The chat room.

ANITA DUNN:

The new news cycle began at 10:00 at night when the [*Washington*] *Post* or the [*New York*] *Times* would actually post their pieces that would be in the paper the next morning. By the time folks like my neighbors who read the paper [read it], we'd be eight news cycles past them. We already would've produced advertising to respond to what was in the paper or we would've made the decision not to respond.

We decided very quickly that we were going to force the media to actually cover the campaign on our terms. We had a reputation, to some extent deserved, for a level of discipline, [for] not leaking. We didn't always have it in the primary but by the general, we'd gotten it down fairly well. Part of that was the decision we made that we would force the coverage to our campaign events, to the things the campaign did and we would not talk about anything else. For instance, we never gave a process interview to the *New York Times*, to either of their very good reporters who cover politics.

I don't think we ever gave the candidate an interview with Adam Nagourney after October 2007. Certainly not on my watch, as we like to say. We tried to force them to cover what was happening as opposed to the back story about what was happening. That was a source of great conflict between us and our press corps. They complained continually about our lack of accessibility but, at the end of the day, forcing them to cover what we wanted them to cover was incredibly important to us.

One of the things that we did was communicate, by and large, most of our news to our supporters. We did that mostly because we really cared about our supporters. When the Clinton people joined the campaign, after the primary was over, one of the most surprising things for them was how much time we spent in meetings talking about how we were going to talk to our supporters about something. In the VP roll-out, the Obama campaign people's starting assumption was that we were going to tell our supporters before we told the press. Clinton people were surprised by the idea that we weren't going to give the story to the AP first after cutting a deal with [AP political reporter] Ron Fournier.

We handled our money announcement in the same way. It was how we did our Invesco [acceptance speech at the Democratic Convention] announcement. David Plouffe would do "hostage-looking" videos [videos akin to those showing hostages pleading for release]. Parenthetically, I'm always surprised when I see that we ended up spending 36.4 million in Florida because in August we did a video to our supporters telling them we were going to spend 39 million there. I'm stunned at how close we came.

When we made the announcement that we were leaving the public financing system, we told our supporters [first].

By September, interviews with national print reporters were nonexistent because there was very little reason at the end of the day to do them. We did national electronic because that's how people get their information. Print does not drive news. Internet drives cable; cable drives networks. If you want a story in the *Post* or the *Times* to drive news, you have to consciously make it a news driver. You produce an ad. You do a conference call. . . .

We actually decided that in light of the scarce time of Barack Obama, our press priorities were battleground states. Everything in our campaign was driven by battleground states.

The third thing, and I think David Plouffe and David Axelrod both alluded to this, when we saw slack times in the primary, we didn't have a problem because there was always another primary, some news-making event, for reporters to cover. During the general, we didn't have that. We had three debates in that big stretch of time. So we needed to create events. That was a big driving force behind our 30-minute program. [We did these things] almost as a way to kill the clock because if we were filling that space, you [in the McCain campaign] weren't. A huge part of what we were trying to do in the general election was to keep you from filling that space. The McCain [campaign] tortured us all summer and we were not happy about that whatsoever.

The place where I think the press [produced] its worst coverage of the general election was in the total absence of any kind of scrutiny of the issue on which we spent the most money in the general election, healthcare. I worked from Chicago. When I started going to battleground states for debate prep, the first state we went to was Florida. That was the first time I'd actually been in a battleground television market, was able to see the amount of advertising we were doing. All we saw in Illinois was national cable. [After watching TV in Florida] I thought, "Oh, my gosh. You see on paper how many advertising dollars are going into markets but it's different being in Tampa and seeing how much money was being spent behind [the issue of] health care."

When we were in Asheville, North Carolina, preparing for the second debate, the number of times I saw the "ball of string and the left-right arrows" health care ad, which anybody who was in a battleground state saw at least 2,000 times, was pretty stunning. The fact is, there was a real health care debate. We brought it up in the debates. John McCain brought it up in the debates. There was a huge difference of opinion. Because, I'm assuming, of financial constraints, you guys didn't advertise on it, you couldn't answer—

NICOLLE WALLACE:

You saw the hybrids?

ANITA DUNN:

This is my parenthesis about the hybrids. In 2004, my firm was part of the John Kerry media team. When the Bush campaign put its first hybrid up, the Kerry people called and were concerned that the Republican lawyers had thought of these hybrids. In 2004 it was cutting edge. In 2008, it's yesterday's—

NICOLLE WALLACE:

It ran its life cycle.

ANITA DUNN:

—life cycle. I thought [the campaigns' emphasis on health care and the national news] was a very good example of how what was going on in the battleground states with voters was almost totally disconnected from the national narrative. [The focus there was on] Bill Ayers and the Sarah Palin interviews. [Meanwhile] there was a whole campaign going on that people [were seeing in our ads] in battleground states, [or hearing when they] were being contacted by Jon Carson's folks. . . .

We actually went back to the model where we communicated about the content we were airing advertising about. Amazing how that actually worked. Local media would cover the issues. That still works out there. You go to Toledo, Ohio, and make a speech about health care, and the Toledo paper and the Toledo TV stations say, "Barack Obama was here today talking about health care" as opposed to, "Barack Obama, who is still reeling from the accusation that his crowd was too big yesterday, came to make a pathetic excuse about why he's not a celebrity."

The final thing I want to address is the question of the referees. I think Joel Benenson mentioned this. Our early focus groups said, "He kind of disagrees with Bush occasionally." But they knew two things about him. One, he was a Republican. And two, he was 71 years old. So a lot to work with there.

In the month of August the celebrity ads really did freak us out. At one point I was screaming about how we were going to be doing our convention chanting dirges, wearing sackcloth and ashes if some had their way. But the fact of the matter is that August was the month where I felt that the referees actually played a significant role in making it difficult, if not impossible, for the McCain campaign to effectively use some of the issues that it wanted to raise about who Barack Obama was personally. I don't know [if those of you in the Republican] campaign consciously decided that you didn't actually care about the editorials and didn't care about the fact checks. But you had a string of things [that suggested to me] that you had made a conscious decision that you didn't care any longer. Or at least that it was not a big voter [concern]. The tax charges against us made a valid point, and then you went ten percent further which gave us the opportunity to "wham you" on the ten percent. At times, we did say [when creating our own material], "Why are we bothering [to be accurate]?" And I think that the Spanish radio ad [on immigration] actually came out of one of those moments. "Why bother? They're not paying any price. They keep running this stuff and nobody cares."

But the fact of the matter is that the job of the referees has changed. In our testing, it was far more credible [with voters] to say that Fact-Check or this independent organization that monitors these things [had said X] as opposed to the *Post* or the *Times* or NBC or any other news org. I don't know if you did [feel so or not] but I did feel at the end of the day that the referees ended up playing a significant role and one that we didn't anticipate coming out of the primaries.

I also want to associate myself with Nicolle's comments about how the press needs to do a lot of soul searching. There was this trivial pursuit. We couldn't believe it.

NICOLLE WALLACE:

I would often get up at three or four and do a round of morning television and answer questions about all the crazy stuff.

ANITA DUNN:

The idiotic stuff.

NICOLLE WALLACE:

I was on the road full time. John McCain did one to three hours of battleground media every day. We didn't do it for the kind of spiritual, meaningful reasons that the Obama campaign did it. Compared to the other campaign, we had no money. We did it because we felt it was important to go around the filter and communicate directly with our voters. So, we did two to three hours of battleground media, I'd say every day from the middle of August until Election Day. That would usually include at least one, sometimes two, satellite tours into target states. Wherever he went, Senator McCain would sit down with three or four network affiliate reporters in a market and the print reporters. So, it was usually five reporters in a local market, plus a sat[ellite] tour, and if we were hitting two states, he'd do that twice.

He'd ask me sometimes, "What'd you get this morning?" And I'd reply, "Nothing that you'll get. I mean, nothing. . . . I promise you, in three hours, you will not get a single question I got." And he never did. Occasionally on Colin Powell—

ANITA DUNN:

If it was a big story—

NICOLLE WALLACE:

If it was a big story, yes. If it was something real people cared out, then he would get it. But if it was something that only cable T.V. hosts were talking about, he would never get the questions I got in the morning, ever. I used to say to my husband that it's like that *Seinfeld* episode where George decides to do the opposite. And I said, "Whatever they're asking about, our position should be the opposite of what they said."

In my first job at the White House in 2001, I ran the Office of Media Affairs, which is the regional press office for all the reporters that don't go to the briefing room every day. Whatever the President did that day, we'd send their way, and the stories were tracked. I am dying to see how that washes out in this White House.

In this campaign, people in the battleground states had a conversation for 15 months about how crappy the economy was. [By contrast] the national media only talked about it for the last six weeks. In Michigan, we were getting questions about their unemployment rate, the state of their economy, and the auto industry for a year. I don't remember the network mix turning to almost purely economy until the last five, six weeks.

ANITA DUNN:

They didn't. We got economic questions during the primary because our primary process went so much longer. But the questions [from the national media focused on] why we weren't connecting better on the economy, as opposed to [concentrating on] the extraordinary amount of policy that we put out. I think we put out more policy [positions] than any campaign ever has. And [we] continually tweaked the policy.

Every morning in the general election, we'd send somebody from our campaign out and the questions would [not only] be ludicrous [but also] would have nothing to do with what we were seeing in any polling.

We would sit down in our Sunday planning meetings and map out the idiotic press ads that we were going to need for the week. One of the things that we discovered was that our regular ads, the ads we were running for voters, weren't covered because [the press didn't consider them] interesting enough. They just worked.

NICOLLE WALLACE:

Too substantive. It is an Alice in Wonderland scenario. I've done this for 12 years. I wouldn't have done this for as long as I have if I didn't really like a lot of people in the media. There are plenty of people in the media who if given a truth serum, would not say things too discordant with what we've said.

ANITA DUNN:

It was like the Wild West out there. . . . I think that part of the reputation we got for being such control freaks was because we simply were trying to control the things we could control. By the general election, we'd figured out how we could game the system to do what we wanted to do and at the same time, keep everybody busy, giving them content to keep 'em busy while you actually went out—

NICOLLE WALLACE:

Like a puppy.

ANITA DUNN:

—and won the campaigns.

JON CARSON:

What's the future of the 30-second ad? I mean, I don't think anyone thinks it's going to be around in 20 years, in 2016, 2012.

ANITA DUNN:

We liked 30-second ads, but we also liked longer form. Obviously the Web allows us to do so much more as well. Thirty-second ads are going to continue to be a part of the mix . . .

NICOLLE WALLACE:

I think that you'll see 30-second ads for a long time. So, not going to die that soon.

CHRIS MOTTOLA:

Do you see local news and blogs becoming the important driving venues? Is network [news] going to become like HBO and Showtime, that you go to for something you want but the real driving force is going to be something else? . . .

ANITA DUNN:

I thought one of the striking things about this campaign was the thirst the people had to make their own judgments as opposed to being told what they should believe about things. . . .

We did a lot of long form stuff. [President-Elect Obama's] better long form. We did a lot of television because it's a good format for him.

Nicolle is absolutely right. By 8:30 in the morning, reporters who were traveling with you had posted a bunch of material and none of it had anything to do with anything. Then the next thing you know you're being asked to respond to that.

[So candidates talk] to the [reporters] who are going to actually allow them to talk about issues. By the end of the campaign, we were very down on morning shows. They had become—

NICOLLE WALLACE:

Yeah. Both campaigns spent a lot a time with *60 Minutes.*

ANITA DUNN:

Right.

NICOLLE WALLACE:

I think—I think—

ANITA DUNN:

And there's a reason why.

NICOLLE WALLACE:

We would be on the same hour. There was certainly no coordinated media strategy, but the networks played, "Well, we've got Obama for the hour. Do you want the . . . " I don't know that we turned down many opportunities to sit down to talk about [substance]. I think *60 Minutes* was one of the winners of the cycle. Both campaigns had relationships there; both campaigns talked to them. And they have a gazillion viewers. On a Sunday night, its appointment television, which means people know it's on. They either TiVo it or they sit and they watch and they listen.

ANITA DUNN:

And it's not as if they were easy interviews.

NICOLLE WALLACE:

No, no.

ANITA DUNN:

They were interviews in which the candidates felt they were actually having a conversation.

NICOLLE WALLACE:

We spent a lot of time with Charlie Gibson. I know you did a few things with Brian Williams and with Gibson.

ANITA DUNN:

And we did Katie Couric. We both did.

NICOLLE WALLACE:

Katie Couric did a lot of stuff with both of our candidates. I think [that sort of interview] will always all be in the mix. And I think that people who have our jobs in the future will put it together around their own mix.

ANITA DUNN:

The news organizations are evolving as well. *U.S. News* has already announced it's going to biweekly, which means it's dying. So they're going to evolve as well. One of the challenges for the news media is making themselves relevant, and a [place] that people want to turn to for information. Increasingly people are searching out news broadcasts that reflect their own opinion. Which I do not believe is healthy, by the way—

NICOLLE WALLACE:

I don't either. And—

ANITA DUNN:

—at all.

NICOLLE WALLACE:

This was the first cycle where each party was largely viewed to have had a cable network in their corner.

ANITA DUNN:

We had one hour and you have an entire network.

NICOLLE WALLACE:

I think that a lot of Republicans feel, these are emotional assessments, not real analysis, that MS(NBC) is hard [on Republicans]. I think it's pretty fair to say that Fox is tough on Democrats. But I can see—

ANITA DUNN:

I think it's fair to say that Fox called Michelle "Barack's baby mama."

NICOLLE WALLACE:

Anyway, my point is, CNN did very well. CNN thrived as the one network that was not associated reputationally with an hour or more of unbalanced coverage. And CNN—

ANITA DUNN:

Although we had a huge issue with CNN during the—

NICOLLE WALLACE:

We did too—

ANITA DUNN:

—primaries.

NICOLLE WALLACE:

—but their ratings soared.

ANITA DUNN:

Because they were seen as more neutral.

NICOLLE WALLACE:

Right. And it's—

ANITA DUNN:

They—

NICOLLE WALLACE:

—all relative in the media. One's too hot, one's too cold, one's just right. And they did well. They are all businesses. CNN saw an advantage and they marketed [themselves] as the one in the middle.

Chapter 7
Political Party Panel

Rich Beeson

Rich Beeson *has been the political director of the Republican National Committee since January 2007. Immediately prior to this, he was a partner at FLS Connect, a political telemarketing firm. Beeson first joined the RNC in 1997 as a regional finance director, and from 1998 until 2005, he was a regional political director. During his tenure in those two positions, his various regions encompassed 21 states.*

I'm here to talk a bit about hybrid ads. We first started doing hybrid ads in 2004 as a way to maximize our television dollars. In 2008, [hybrid ads] allowed Senator McCain and his campaign to essentially split the cost of advertising with the Republican National Committee. Again, they're called 50–50s, which is exactly what it sounds like; we could split the costs of the spots 50 percent each. It allowed for significantly more television advertising. When you're up against a campaign that had $746 million, you try to figure out everything [you can do to] maximize your television advertising.

How are these ads different? They always have to have a reference to some generic group. It always sounded odd on the radio or on a telephone ad or a telephone spot or a television ad when you heard about the congressional liberals but that's what it took to satisfy the legal requirements.

These are the spot counts. The RNC ran RNC-specific ads about 21 percent of the time, McCain 45 percent of the time, and then the hybrid ads were about 32 percent of the time. So that gives you an idea of how we split the advertising up.

We've got a spot we were going to show before we go into the spending by percentage.

TV Advertisement—"Ambition"

ANNOUNCER: Obama's blind ambition. When convenient he worked with terrorist Bill Ayers. When discovered, he lied.

CHART 22. Spot Count by Percent

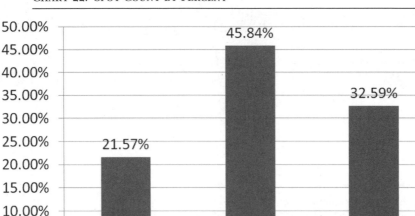

Obama: blind ambition, bad judgment. Congressional liberals fought for risky sub-prime loans. Congressional liberals
fought against more regulation. Then the healthy market collapsed, costing you billions. In crisis, we need leadership, not
bad judgment.

JOHN MCCAIN: I'm John McCain, and I approve this message.

GRAPHIC: Paid for by McCain-Palin 2008 and the Republican
National Committee. Approved by John McCain.

There's no reference in there to Barack Obama; it's a reference to the
congressional liberals. So it allowed the RNC to pay for half of that spot
[and] the McCain campaign to use Senator McCain's image then pay
half of his spot as well. We have one more we're going to show.

TV Advertisement—"Unethical"

ANNOUNCER: Obama rewards his friends with your tax dollars—Tony Rezko, 14 million; Allison Davis, 20 million;
Kenny Smith, 100,000. That's unethical. Congressional liberals promised to raise your taxes to reward their friends with
wasteful pork—taxes for you, pork for them. Who's going to
stop them, congressional liberals or him?

CHART 23. ESTIMATED AD SPENDING BY PERCENT

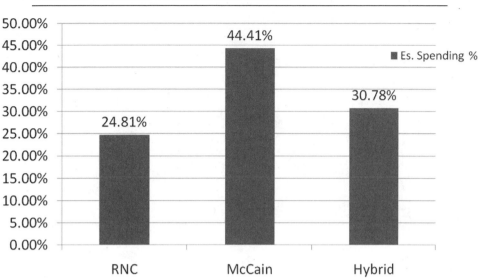

JOHN MCCAIN: I'm John McCain and I approve this message.

GRAPHIC: Paid for by McCain-Palin 2008 and the Republican National Committee. Approved by John McCain.

That gives you an idea of what the hybrid ads look like. Clearly, the best television spots to run are the straight campaign spots, whether it's John McCain specifically or whether it's an anti-Obama spot. Those are the best spots. That's where the Obama campaign had the distinct advantage. By raising $746 million, they were able to go up with direct television spots: "I'm Barack Obama, I approve this message." It was Obama to camera. It was direct negative spots on McCain. Those are the cleanest and best spots. But in order to maximize what resources we had, we had to be creative. [But when using hybrid ads] you don't get as clean a hit as you do with a straight candidate ad.

This gives you an idea of the spot count by percentage in various states.

You can see how the mix was different depending on the state. In as many states as possible, the McCain ads should be the highest number of all. But in states like Florida, where spending was enormous, the RNC and the hybrid ads were the bulk of the spending. So it varied by state and it was a calculated strategy [to the extent to which there is] a calculated strategy when you have limited amounts of resources and [are] trying to spread them around as effectively as possible.

CHART 24. SPOT COUNT BY PERCENT IN VARIOUS STATES

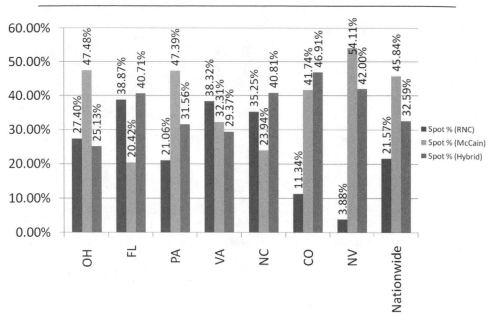

This slide gives you an idea on the spot by percentage in each state. Hybrid ads gave us an ability to stretch our ad buys, to essentially double the number of spots by splitting the cost and doing a 50–50 and having twice as many spots.

We brought a knife to a gun fight and we had to do everything that we could do to maximize the resources we had. The hybrid ads were one effective way. We had coordinated spending. We had independent expenditure spending. And then we had the McCain campaign. At the end of the day, we were overwhelmed by the number, just the pure number of spots.

Karen Finney

Karen Finney is director of communications of the Democratic National Committee. She joined the DNC staff in 2005, helping shape the messages that contributed to Democratic victories in the 2006 midterm elections and in the 2008 campaigns. Previously, she was director of communications for Elizabeth Edwards during the 2004 Kerry/Edwards presidential campaign, and in 2000 she was press secretary for Hillary Clinton's successful campaign for the U.S. Senate in New York. Finney entered politics working on the Clinton/Gore campaign advance team in 1992, and later served for several years in the White House.

The DNC did television ads; we did robocalls; we did print advertising; we did radio ads. But one of the things that Governor Dean, when he came into the DNC, believed was that as a party we were spending a lot of money on television ads and that the impact of television advertising was diminishing as media becomes more fractured.

In 2005 we looked at a number of trends, as we started to think about our strategy going forward. Part of the 50-state strategy was not just putting staff on the ground but also rebuilding our technological infrastructures. We know voters are more likely to respond to information that comes from a trusted source. This is one of the places where we were, frankly, outmaneuvered in 2004, where the Republicans were better able to have people from local communities knocking on doors [while] we were busing people in from other places.

Also, we know that changes in media and technology give voters more control over how and where they are getting their information. You don't have to watch the evening news. You can TiVo it and decide what portion of the evening news you're going to watch. You can go to blogs or Web sites. We also knew that if we could effectively harness technology, we could do more effective message targeting.

The last piece, a lesson learned from the Dean campaign: online activity doesn't always translate into offline activity. That was certainly one of the challenges that they [the Dean campaign] faced. There was a lot of energy online, they were very successful in raising money online, but they weren't able to motivate people, whether it was the message or the actual tools, to then get people who were online to do what we needed them to do offline, which was to vote.

A quick look at what's changing in political communication. Cable and TiVo reduce the impact of television commercials. An estimated 33 percent of households will have DVR machines by the end of 2008. So when you're looking at how you're going to spend your TV ad dollars, that's one of the things we're thinking about. Satellite radio and MP3 players are lessening the impact of radio advertising. Caller ID and cell phones are making it harder to reach people through robocalls. About one in seven adults uses only cell phones and one in five adults has no landline. We think that trend obviously is going to continue. We know also, younger voters don't tend to read their mail. . . . Those dollars are wasted on people like me who throw it out.

Knowing that this is the landscape, how can we more effectively reach and persuade voters? Governor Dean believed that the way to do it was through the grassroots. This is a composite our political folks put together looking at the number of contacts needed to move a vote.

We built the neighbor to neighbor tool. Essentially it sits on top of our voter file and engages activists. Instead of walking into a campaign office

CHART 25. EFFICIENCY OF GRASSROOTS POLITICAL STRATEGY

Contacts Needed for Just One Additional Vote	
Mail	389
Phone	460
Canvass	14

and being handed a stack of flyers to go hand out or a sign to go hold over a highway, you can actually do something meaningful that helps to move votes. We also developed the system in a way that [allows] candidates and state parties to target their message and, as we do micro-targeting, we can more effectively figure out, is it nurses, is it women, is it veterans, where are they, how do we reach them. Person-to-person contact has that element of familiarity between the two people.

The Obama campaign built MyBO; after Obama became the nominee, we were able to merge the two systems into one.

We looked at some research by the Consortium of Behavioral Scientists when we were developing our GOTV scripts. In the scripts you talk about making a voting plan. If people have a plan, they're more likely to get out and vote. You talk about an expected record turnout. People want to be a part of a record turnout. It's going to make you feel good. You're going to want to be a part of it. You want to assist people: do you know where your polling location is? How are you going to get there—again, trying to start to lower some of those mental barriers to actually motivate someone to get out to vote, bringing others to the polls and then the last piece—matching callers to respondents. As much as possible, in the door-to-door activity and on the phone we matched up veterans calling veterans [for example]. We find that's more effective.

The other thing you can do is print materials from your computer. These materials were developed nationally. They could be customized, though, at the state level. If in Ohio jobs is the leading issue, [the material could be tailored] so that that was the leading issue. Or if it was Colorado where some of the land use and water issues were targeted, you could make those changes, in both the script and the materials. You could also print the materials in Spanish. So we've deputized individual citizens to be our messengers and carry our message. And in essence, an individual is re-branding the Obama-Biden campaign in his neighborhood in a way that you can't do with a television ad, you can't do with a radio spot, you can't do with a robocall. We think that is a more meaningful contact with the voter than the impressions you get from the advertising.

There are things built into the system to motivate people to reach their goals. All the data come back to us and to our vote-builder system. We found that the data we get back from this system are actually better, in some instances, than [from] the paid canvassers. The information that people give you about their neighbors and their voting habits is actually in some ways better. All of that helps us as we're doing our micro-targeting and looking to how we do our messaging more effectively.

Finally, we ask you to recruit your friends, and that's how we build our system all across the country. Between August and Election Day, there were over 125,000 active users. They made over 6 million calls or knocks, which was a mean of about 51 calls or knocks per person. On Election Day, the activists were making about 286 calls per second in the system.

The majority of the people used the scripts that we provided; some rewrote the scripts to customize them, some did a mix of the scripts. We also did what we called micro-campaigns. When you came into the system you could say if you were a Spanish speaker, if you were a woman willing to make calls to other women, if you were a veteran. If you are a Latino we would match you up and give you a call list of Latinos. If you're in Nevada and you want to call Latinos in Colorado [we would do the same]. Again, we felt that that person-to-person, shared experience, shared background was effective. . . .

We believe in the end that personal contact actually moves votes. A CBS [poll reported] 26 percent of voters were contacted by Obama during the campaign, compared to 19 percent by the McCain campaign.[1] Obama received 65 percent of support among those voters who were contacted by his campaign compared to 47 percent from those who weren't. So we thought that this was an important part of the mix.

BROOKS JACKSON, FACTCHECK.ORG:

When I first came to Washington, the Republican Party had a technological edge in terms of voter files, the ability to categorize voters and cross voters by driver's license data and all sorts of other stuff. . . . How would you say the RNC's effort compared to what you just saw Karen present? Have they leapfrogged over you in technology now?

RICH BEESON:

There are two parts to that. One is the technology, the other is the data. And I think that one thing that the RNC has done a very good job at over the last 20 years is the data management of voter files. We have 183 million voter file records in our basement. We have pinned every bit of information we can ever find to those voter files, whether its micro-targeting data, whether its ID data. This year, in the last 19 weeks of the campaign, our volunteers made 30 million contacts, both phones and knocks. Every one of those contacts was uploaded into the system and appended to the file. So with the micro-targeting data, you're also appending consumer data to the file. I'd put our data up against anybody's. As for the technology, what the Obama campaign was able to do this cycle was groundbreaking. But they do have a ways to go on the data front I think.

BROOKS JACKSON:

We [at FactCheck.org] love TV ads because they're 30 seconds and we can monitor them; we know we can take them off the air. We have no ability to monitor what your neighbors are saying to other neighbors. And I'm just wondering what sort of messages get transmitted there and what we might be missing.

KAREN FINNEY:

What you're getting is that personal flavor and that personal opinion. We think that when people put their own personal spin on it or their personal take on it, that is a more effective message and communication. We can't monitor it, which is why I think for some time there was some reluctance to give more power to the grassroots. [To do that] you actually have to trust that when that person knocks on the door, they're going to deliver the message that you have in the script or on the walk materials. We've tried to create a system with as much control as we can but we share the same challenge.

BROOKS JACKSON:

I wonder if you could talk about how much money went into this neighbor-to-neighbor versus television advertising you might have done in the presidential primaries?

KAREN FINNEY:

During the general election the DNC didn't do television advertising; it was predominantly done by the Obama campaign.

This system [cost over] $10–12 million [to build]. We started in 2005 by looking at what the Republicans were able to do. When Governor Dean became chairman, we didn't have a national voter file. We weren't able to do micro-targeting in the way that the Republicans were. So a lot of the money went into building a national voter file, getting it up and running in every state, training voter file managers, just getting the basics and developing our own methods of micro-targeting, which we tested in 2006 and 2007 so that we could be ready. Technology moves so fast, we weren't necessarily trying to build to where the RNC was in 2004. We were able to build to best of breed, looking forward to 2008 and beyond. What you can do with information [in 2012] will be leaps and bounds from where we are now.

BROOKS JACKSON:

How staff intensive was it? How many paid staff had to be devoted to running this system?

KAREN FINNEY:

I would say 20 or 30 people in our IT department and our political department. We'd had a cross departmental team working on it so that we were developing not just from the technological standpoint but also from the political standpoint. From the user interface standpoint we wanted it to be as easy as possible for people to use. My mother who was a volunteer in Maryland actually called me—she was so excited [that] it was so easy to use. So we used a cross-divisional approach to make sure that we were meeting everybody's specifications.

BROOKS JACKSON:

Rich, the hybrid ad strategy allowed you to spend more money on John McCain's campaign. Just so the point doesn't get lost, of course he was subject to spending limits. How much were you able to, by the use of hybrid ads, expand the spending limits, in effect, for John McCain? How many extra dollars went into advertising as a result of hybrid ads?

RICH BEESON:

I don't have the exact number. It was around 50 million, roughly, in directed. The RNC could do 19.2 million in coordinated, which is essentially that much money in additional television.

BROOKS JACKSON:

Those coordinated ads looked just like John McCain ads and didn't have to talk about liberals in Congress or anything like that, right.

RICH BEESON:

Exactly with a different disclaimer. So around 50 million extra. Again, I don't know if I've mentioned this, but the Obama campaign had $746 million—(LAUGHTER)—and so when you're talking those sorts of numbers, it really paled in comparison.

BROOKS JACKSON:

How effective were those hybrid ads? Did you focus group [test] them, did you test afterward? We've heard complaints from the McCain folks that [the hybrid ads were] incomprehensible and [they] stopped doing them because they weren't working.

RICH BEESON:

Well, it's weight of message. I said in my monologue that the cleanest ad is a candidate ad that gets up and says "vote for or vote against," "paid for by"—those are the best sort of ads. When the lawyers get involved in the hybrid ads, they certainly are watered down. Are they the perfect spots? No, not at all. But when you're trying to get a weight of message and a certain number of spots up and that's the best you can do, those are what we had to live with. I understand that when you're talking about congressional liberals, it's an amorphous term that's a lot less effective than saying "Governor Blagojevich has some serious issues."

BROOKS JACKSON:

So were there focus groups or [is there] any quantifiable data you could share with us?

RICH BEESON:

I've sat in on focus groups across the country with a number of different groups and there were a lot of different messages that tested very well. But again, I keep coming back to two points, that if you can't have a clean hit in the spot and you're getting literally 80-to-one on spots, it makes it a little difficult to burn a message in.

KATHLEEN HALL JAMIESON, ANNENBERG PUBLIC POLICY CENTER:

Karen, you mentioned the DNC didn't do any television ads; did it do any radio ads?

KAREN FINNEY:

We didn't. All the ads came out of the Obama campaign. We did actually two television ads when the primary was still going on. Then once Obama became the nominee, all the ad dollars came out of the campaign.

KATHLEEN HALL JAMIESON:

Did any messaging come from DNC other than what you described here? Was there direct mail?

KAREN FINNEY:

We did mail out of the DNC and then we did the grassroots materials out of the DNC.

KATHLEEN HALL JAMIESON:

Could you tell us a little bit about the direct mail and did you do any robocalling?

KAREN FINNEY:

We didn't do robocalls out of the DNC. We did a pretty vigorous mail program out of the DNC again with both a persuasion message and then a get-out-to-vote message. But most of our emphasis was really on the system.

RICH BEESON:

With all due respect to my friend Karen, the DNC stood for "Do Not Call" when it came to the Obama campaign. They [the Obama team] had enough resources to run their entire operation out of their campaign and it was clear that they did. You saw cash-on-hand figures. In September, the RNC was at 76 million and the DNC was at 17 million. The Obama campaign made a conscious effort to run their entire operation out of their campaign.

KAREN FINNEY:

Between our two campaigns, when you talked about 30 million calls in the last 19 weeks, we were able to make 68 million calls in that same time period, so resources helped.

KATHLEEN HALL JAMIESON:

And Rich, did you distribute your hybrid ads into radio and television and if so, what was the mix and into what states?

RICH BEESON:

The states were up on the slide [see Chart 24].

It was radio, it was television, it was calls. We did it as much as possible. We tried to spread it out. I think we were at one point in thirty-six different states. Clearly, we were fighting on fronts we didn't necessarily want to be fighting on. The Obama campaign did a very good job of keeping us moving around the country and playing in states that we would have preferred not to be running ads in.

QUESTION:

During every campaign I seem to see, through the backwaters, certain rumors pop up. And they're different depending on which campaign it is—things like Obama was born in Kenya, Sarah Palin's baby, things like that that come up through chat rooms on the internet. You can recognize them immediately because it's a cut-and-paste message. What I want to ask of you two is "Do your organizations have skunk-works in the back somewhere that generate these things and try to get them distributed?"

RICH BEESON:

Tell him the truth!

KAREN FINNEY:

(CHUCKLES) I'm sure I don't know what you're talking about. No, go ahead Rich—you go first.

RICH BEESON:

Anything that was a rumor certainly would come out of the DNC. Anything that was a fact would come out of the RNC. I think we can all agree to that. No, sir. That [viral rumors] is one thing that the blogosphere has created. Literally, everybody can now be a journalist. And so you see this stuff pop up all over the place. You never once saw the RNC talking about President-elect Obama's citizenship. That was just not something we ever talked about. We knew that that issue had been settled long ago.

BROOKS JACKSON:

I covered money and politics for many years. When I came to town in the Nixon era, Republicans had a big advantage. Those who could write million or $2 million checks were more often Republicans than not. Once campaign donation limits came into effect, Republicans maintained a big financial advantage, primarily through the ability to raise small dollars. Those fundraising letters from Ronald Reagan brought in tidal waves of cash and the Republican Party enjoyed a financial advantage election after election after election. My question to both of you is "What happened?" The advantage seems to have shifted to the Democrats. Are Democrats richer, have Republicans gotten poorer?

RICH BEESON:

As far as the donor file, you are exactly right. For a long time, the DNC was not a small-donor committee. It was a large-donor committee and did not have a small-donor file. The RNC's average contribution has been around $67. We have about two million donors. The DNC is getting better at that.

The second track of that is large contributions into the 527s—whether it's George Soros or David Geffen, any number of people who write the size of checks that Republican donors just don't match. So they caught up on that front and surpassed [us].

KAREN FINNEY:

I don't think you can quite say they weren't big checks going into 527s on the other side. I have to take issue with that. I think certainly winning helps. In the aftermath of 2000, [Democratic] donors realized that we needed to change the way we're raising money if we were going to win. Winning in 2006 motivated people to believe we could win.

Traditionally, the RNC was better at having institutional givers of the large checks than the DNC was. We found ourselves in a cycle where our big donors would give closer to the cycle and not throughout the years. Part of the argument we made to people was, "You've got to give in the off years because we can't wait until the election is here. We've got to build a voter file, we've got to build ground troops, and we need resources to do that." Having a business plan that you can take to donors was very helpful in [accomplishing] that.

Obviously, the Obama campaign took it to a whole new level. I think people felt that the money was actually going toward something that was effective, efficient and worthy of their time and money. So I think that made a big difference.

BROOKS JACKSON:

A new thing is the "Donate Now" button that you see on every candidate's Web site, every party Web site. Does the ease with which people can make a small donation to a candidate or a political party through the Internet favor one party over another?

KAREN FINNEY:

I don't know that it favors one over the other. There's a psychological element if you send an e-mail that is timely and the action step is donate now. If you're talking about $5, $10, you're lowering that mental barrier to people who say, "I don't have $1,000 to give. I don't even have $100 to give." I think it's the psychology of engaging people and getting them to take an action step.

RICH BEESON:

If there's a good idea that one party has [during] one cycle, the other party will steal it for the next one. We've done that cycle to cycle. The online fundraising by the Obama campaign is legendary right now. What you'll see on our side is increased emphasis on that. What we're looking at is recurring donors, so that over the course of the year, they're giving a lot more than they could ever write with one check. But setting it up on a recurring basis. Online really helps us do that. And so you're seeing a significant focus on the online fundraising, now.

QUESTION:

Is the amount of money taken in really the result of public discontent or is it the result of the fundraising activity?

KAREN FINNEY:

Part of what Governor Dean understood in terms of Internet fundraising is it's not just an ATM. People really want to feel like they're part of a community. Engaging people, and making them feel like they're getting a little bit of an inside look into the campaign or they're really a part of something bigger will make you far more successful with fundraising online. So I think that's part of the puzzle.

I don't think that the McCain campaign did as well as the Obama campaign in engaging people in a movement. Obama's message was a message of change, a message [saying] we can do this together. McCain had the more traditional message "I'm going to fix your problems for you." This message didn't connect with voters. This is why I say strategy is as much a part of it as money. He certainly could have done more to distance himself from Bush if he chose to. And he tried to do that in the general but after trying to run closer to him in the primary, it's harder to then come back to the middle in the general election.

RICH BEESON:

Specifically talking about fundraising, you have to take the good with the bad. The president raised over a billion dollars for the RNC in his tenure. That's not something that we are just going to walk away from and say, "Sorry, you're unpopular." He was still a very, very good fundraiser with our base and raised a significant amount of money to the tune of $67 million over the last couple of years as well. So obviously, the public polling was not very favorable to the president and the McCain campaign had to be cognizant of that. But as far as the base in fundraising, he was still a very good fundraiser.

JOE DAVIDSON, *WASHINGTON POST*:

I wonder if you run the danger of turning off people when it comes to fundraising. I ask that because I have a friend who donated to the Obama campaign and then was constantly inundated with requests for more money to the point where she seemed to be becoming really turned off. I mean it's not like she decided to vote for McCain because you guys asked her for too much money. But it seemed [as if] you had gone beyond the point of diminishing returns.

KAREN FINNEY:

There's always a tension between how much is too much and how much is enough. We talk about burning the lists which tends to happen toward the end where you get not just e-mails on a daily but almost an hourly basis with some new ask. There's the tension between doing it because some people will give and knowing that some people might be turned off. But, as you say, they're probably not going to not vote for your candidate. They might be a little bit turned off by the repetitive asks. After the election you bring it down a bit to give people a little relief.

RICH BEESON:

I would say the key to fundraising is found in the Bible. In the Book of
John, it says, "Ask and you shall receive." It's up to us to give them every
opportunity to do that. Once they have shown a propensity to give, those
are the folks that are more likely to give. An average donor will give to
the RNC three to four times a year. We can't pick what three or four
times that's going to be. We just have to give them multiple opportunities to take advantage of that three to four times a year.

  We're not the only ones in the mix. There are Senate committees, our
congressional committees, our candidates, our outside organizations
that you're going to hear from today. There are so many people out
there asking for money that if you're not in that stream and in that mix,
you run the risk of not getting that person's check. That's a risk that we
can't take.

BROOKS JACKSON:

In this campaign, there was more of the kind of fact-checking journalism
that we do than I've ever seen in any previous campaign. Another Web
site started up by the *St. Petersburg Times*, Politifact.com, the *Washington
Post* weighed in, as did other news organizations. As you and your parties
were crafting their messages, did that make any difference? And if so,
why?

RICH BEESON:

Well, you start off from the premise that what you're saying is true so I
guess you have to assume that it's going to pass a fact-check muster. I
don't recall ever sitting in a meeting with anybody saying, "Let's put
something out there that's going to get smacked back in our face. So do
you try to make it as egregious as possible?" I guess I'm not entirely sure
how to answer it other than "what we say, we always back up." We have
a research department that backs up everything that we put out with
documentation. Our lawyers don't let us put out any mail, any television,
any distribution of any material that can't be backed up with facts.

KAREN FINNEY:

That doesn't mean you don't stretch the truth. I mean we did—
(CHUCKLES)—we actually started something at the DNC during the
campaign, we count the lies [coming from the other side]. And we actually got up to over a hundred. But certainly, I don't know that we sit and

think, "Okay, what are the fact-checkers going to say?" In this campaign each side [was] trying to keep track of how many Pinocchios [each side received in the *Washington Post*]. I will say that it was an important part of the campaign and important to the campaign to really try to fight this battle on the issues and stay as close to the truth and stay as close to the issues and [away from] personal attacks as possible.

Note

1. CBS News Poll, November 11, 2008. "Americans Look Ahead with Optimism," http://www.cbsnews.com/htdocs/pdf/NOV08B-postelection.pdf.

Chapter 8

Democratic/Liberal Panel

Ricky Feller

Ricky Feller *is associate director of the political action department at the American Federation of State, County and Municipal Employees (AFSCME) international union. He is responsible for the oversight of all aspects of the union's political programs, including member mobilization and general public voter contact. Feller worked for presidential, gubernatorial, senatorial, state legislative, county executive, mayoral, and coordinated campaigns prior to his tenure at AFSCME. He also held positions in the federal and state governments.*

I ran AFSCME's independent expenditure program, which included not just presidential, but extensive issue and express advocacy in many states and congressional districts. The first rule for an independent expenditure is do no harm. That means do no harm to the organization you're working for and do no harm to the campaign you're trying to help.

The second rule is to understand that you're not the campaign. You are an assist person. You're going to go in there to help fill a lane. So the first order of business was [identifying] the lanes that we needed to fill. In this case, I'm going to talk more about the presidential and where Barack Obama needed help. We were going to go into two states, one that we needed to keep that we had won in 2004, and one that we needed to pick up that we had lost in 2004.

We were going to go in with substantial resources, filling that lane and spending a good amount of money serving that purpose. We came up with New Mexico and Wisconsin based on extensive tracking [of] what the campaigns, the parties, and other independent expenditures were doing on TV, on radio, on the ground. We also did polling and focus groups. We knew where, of the top 20 markets, the campaigns and others were spending. . . .

McCain was also buying extensively in El Paso, which wasn't really to move any vote in Texas. That was clearly for New Mexico. We had done a lot of polling. Let me just talk about New Mexico first, a place that Gore had won, Kerry lost. We saw [among Latinos], based on early polling [that] Obama was running slightly ahead of Kerry but way behind where Gore had ended up. We were concerned about that. . . . Early on, the numbers just weren't good. Obama was trailing among New Mexico Latinos more than in Nevada and Colorado and in New Mexico, the Latino community's a much larger part of the electorate than in Nevada and Colorado. So we were seeing some signs of trouble early on.

Obama was also trailing at that point among the generic Democratic match-up. So we decided we needed to talk to folks in the Latino communities. We did some more polling later on and among the general public there. Obama was only plus two without the leaners. So we need to pump up that Latino vote. At this point the [Democratic] Senate candidate was running sixteen points ahead. So clearly, there was an issue there. We did some focus groups and particularly among Latino men, the focus group showed that not just is there an economy message out there, but when you start going after McCain on veterans' issues, his strength, it started moving some of this vote away from him.

So we figured everyone in there is talking about the economy, the economy, the economy. Let's fill a lane. . . . We happened to come across something in, I think it might have been in The Hill. It was talking about a group called the Iraq and Afghanistan Veterans of America. They had given him a D for some of his votes so we decided to use that in one of our spots. It's called "Veterans."

TV Advertisement—"Veterans"

SERGEANT DOUGLAS GIBSON: On the tough votes, McCain hasn't been there for veterans.

SEAMAN ROMEO ROCHA: John McCain sided with George Bush and opposed the new G.I. Bill. He opposed full college tuition for new veterans.

JAMES COCHRAN, ARMY: When John McCain has to choose between his party and better care for veterans, he sides with his party.

SGT. DOUGLAS GIBSON: John McCain hasn't voted for us for years. I can't vote for him in November.

ANNOUNCER: AFSCME People is responsible for the content of this advertising.

GRAPHIC: Paid for by American Federation of State, County & Municipal Employees People Committee (202–429–1000). Not authorized by any candidate or candidate's committee.

ASFCME People is responsible for the content of this advertising.

We ran this in Albuquerque, in Amarillo, and in El Paso. We had an extensive buy in those three areas. The New Mexico exit polls will show Latinos ended up being close to 40 percent of the vote. While it really helped move Latinos, Latino men in particular, it was also helpful among the general public. So again, going back to the original "Do no harm," this was doing no harm with the general public and was going after the niche vote that we were looking for. So among Latinos, overall, in New Mexico, Obama did better than he did nationally. Among Latino men, he did better in New Mexico than he did nationally among Latino men.

The next state we were in is Wisconsin. That's a state that was a small margin win [and] a state that we needed to keep. We polled extensively there [and found] Obama with a slight margin. He was within the margin of error. Later on in the fall . . . he had actually lost some ground there. So we decided to go in and do a little more fine polling. Obama was doing well, naturally, in the Milwaukee area. He was weak in Green Bay and other areas.

Particularly of concern were the Independents, who make up roughly 30 percent of the vote. Independents were basically dead even, which cut both ways. It was good and bad at that point in the campaign. So we decided . . . to slice off a piece and go after niche and not go into Milwaukee that much. We were going into some of these other areas because polls and focus groups showed swing voters would be coming out of Green Bay, the northeast, downscale men, true Independents, not Independents who lean Democrat or lean Republican, and women, older women as well.

We decided to use the economic message and link it with Social Security and Medicare. We did come across Club for Growth espousing McCain's position on Social Security. This is a spot called "Security."

TV Advertisement—"Security"

SR. MALE: I'm on a fixed income.

SR. FEMALE: And so am I.

MALE: What would my folks do without Social Security?

FEMALE: Why does John McCain support privatizing Social Security?

MALE: He wants to put it into Wall Street's hands. What is he thinking?

SR. MALE 2: I'm surprised he's that out of touch.

SR. FEMALE: You could wake up one day and the money would all be gone.

SR. MALE: We earned that money. Now, he wants to give it to Wall Street. (Chorus of, "No way.")

ANNOUNCER: AFSCME People is responsible for the content of this advertising.

GRAPHIC: Paid for by American Federation of State, County & Municipal Employees People Committee (202–429–1000). Not authorized by any candidate or candidate's committee. ASFCME People is responsible for the content of this advertising.

Now, these were all real people [in both the Wisconsin and New Mexico ads]. So this spot was not only for our targeted audience, but would do well in general.

In the exit polls, we did better in Wisconsin [by eight points than] nationally among voters 50–64 years old. Now, we all know that he lost among seniors, right? But he was actually dead even in Wisconsin. And among Independents, he was plus six in Wisconsin than he was nationally. So our stuff was effective. We made some very targeted buys. We were on for a good amount of time. We did some good polling, focus groups. And going back to the original rule of an IE [independent expenditure], fill a lane. Based on results, I think we had a successful campaign.

Lawrence Scanlon

Lawrence Scanlon is director of the political action department at the American Federation of State, County and Municipal Employees. He started his career in the union in 1974 as a field representative for the 250,000-member New York Civil Service Employees Association, AFSCME Local 1000. He held a series of positions with the union and was appointed executive director in 1992. In 1995, President Gerald W. McEntee tapped Scanlon to direct AFSCME's political department. His responsibilities for the 1.6 million-member union include the development and implementation of the union's political strategy to support candidates and campaigns (federal, state, and local) that will positively impact public policy and union-member issues.

I'm the political director for AFSCME, the American Federation of State, County and Municipal Employees. We represent about 1.6 million members in every state and the Commonwealth of Puerto Rico. We have a very active political program. Ricky has detailed some of the work that he's done in terms of the Independent expenditures. If we think back to some of the changes in the laws, the rules, the regulations, you think back to BCRA [Bipartisan Campaign Reform Act]. I thought it was interesting that the Republican Rich Beeson didn't mention that BCRA is the McCain-Feingold Act. So [when] you talk about being hoist on your own petard, this is the case.

We had changes in the FEC regulations and we had the Wisconsin Supreme Court decision in the Right to Life case.[1] The ground shifts and you have to be very nimble, opportunistic, and creative when you're doing your political programs if you want your candidates to win.

Our union is led by Gerald McEntee. He's been in the labor movement, now, 50 years. He also serves as the chair of the AFL-CIO political committee and as such, helps drive that program. So I'm going to present some data regarding the AFL program as well.

Our union is very active. Over the cycle from '07 to '08, we spent $84.2 million on politics. That's hard dollars and soft dollars. We had an unusual circumstance in that we did not support Barack Obama in the primaries. This process, for us, started in January of 2007 when Senator Reid called and asked us if we would host the first presidential forum for Democratic candidates in Carson City, Nevada. My comment was, "Oh, just shoot me, okay? But yeah, sure, we'll do it." We went through an exhaustive process to screen all the candidates [and] made our endorsement of Senator Hillary Clinton on October 31, 2007.

We worked very hard for her. On June 3, the race is basically over and so all the work that we had done with our membership in terms of educating them on the differences with the candidates and why they should support Hillary Clinton, now [required that] we had to shift gears and go through a whole other education program. . . .

Here is just a brief composite of what we did. We put 455 staff out into the 17 battleground states. We made 7 million phone calls overall to our members. We did a nonpartisan turnout program [and] over a million pieces of mail in the general election. We did nonpartisan work, which is driving voters to the polls on a nonpartisan basis. "It's their civic duty to get out and vote." We did that in New Mexico and Florida and Wisconsin. In other places, we did voter protection, election protection [New Mexico, Florida, Wisconsin, Virginia]. We had attorneys out working making sure that people had the right to vote and their vote was actually counted.

Our polling showed that the economy was the most important issue for our members. Public polling shows that [that was] the most important issue. But Social Security is very important to our members, economic security is important to them. The McCain health care plan would actually be a tax increase for working families, to the tune of

$2,800. You saw the previous ad that talked about the fact that he wanted to privatize Social Security, which actually, in our judgment, was the beginning of the end of the Bush administration. He [President George W. Bush] came out of the 2004 election and said "I'm going to use my political capital, I'm going to get this rammed through." When it didn't happen, he lost whatever capital that he had.

The AFL program went into 22 battleground states. The AFL represents roughly 10 million people in the country.

In Ohio, Pennsylvania, and Michigan, very dense union states, we always have to fight and scrape for every vote. Ohio, we flipped this time. Pennsylvania, we won going away. Michigan, I thought was crucial. [Among] the strategic mistakes that the McCain campaign made [was] announcing that they were pulling out of Michigan in early October. I was very concerned about Michigan because of the economic problems and I didn't know whether it was going to be a referendum on [Democratic Governor] Jennifer Granholm or on the Republicans. Fortunately, it turned out to be referendum on the Republicans.

The AFL sent out a lot of mail. One was the negative piece undercutting McCain with our members and the other was a positive piece that introduced Senator Obama to our members. . . . [The AFL] embarked on a very aggressive campaign in the spring and early summer to all union members saying "Here's the real John McCain. He's not the maverick that you think he is. Here's what his record is on economics and on jobs and on trade and on social security." They did a very effective job in basically ruining his brand.

That's important because, if you look at the early polling from February, AFL union households were remarkably similar to the public in terms of their favorable opinion of McCain. So we all knew at that point we had a very high mountain to climb. And so we did a lot of worksite flyers. We find that the most important way to communicate with members is face-to-face. That's how we raise our political money, it's how we get our message out. Unions are trusted messengers. Karen Finney mentioned that as one of her points in her presentation. Our leadership is trusted because we've proven that we're speaking the truth to power, if you will, with our members.

How did the union members vote? 67–30 for Obama, a 37-point margin and the general public basically was 51–47. The exit polls ended up 53–47. In the battleground states, because there was more attention there, we did even better with union members voting by a 69–28 margin. The big swings were age 65, which McCain did very well with general voters compared to the other categories. But we helped carry union older voters for Barack Obama.

Now, for the past three cycles, you'll see that union members per-

CHART 26. AFL MEMBER CONTACT PROGRAM NUMBERS IN 22 BATTLEGROUND
STATES

State	Mail	Doorknocks	Worksite Contacts	Phone
OH	11,113,743	2,631,713	5,245,508	16,298,492
PA	7,315,261	2,376,485	4,69,373	12,371,919
MI	5,823,307	1,414,615	2,807,817	8,31,438
WI	3,815,644	985,466	1,468,656	5,196,743
MN	3,506,122	974,304	1,528,785	5,031,443
FL	3,154,363	884,440	1,932,993	4,144,424
IN	3,036,165	577,702	1,681,673	2,708,177
MO	1,951,142	483,543	991,552	2,607,247
WA	3,025,027	211,650	1,300,573	1,485,179
OR	1,378,060	402,024	513,361	1,914,351
KY	1,363,051	206,475	828,252	1,501,486
VA	1,208,957	320,127	914,409	1,345,430
CO	1,020,627	319,024	516,839	1,437,162
GA	770,851	191,036	391,739	1,030,062
NC	684,505	169,638	347,859	914,681
NM	570,287	194,090	228,264	890,660
IA	602,428	149,297	306,148	805,004
NV	321,770	79,743	163,520	429,971
ME	266,906	66,146	135,639	356,658
NH	247,740	97,090	110,928	272,776
MS	275,460	54,646	159,892	149,111
AK	202,542	60,772	43,019	181,907
Other BG ODs	3,640,627	902,240	1,850,132	4,864,849
Non-BG states	1,488,335	146,188	789,006	1,331,612
TOTALS	56,782,920	13,898,454	28,865,937	75,582,782

CHART 27. AFSCME SUPPORT OVER TIME

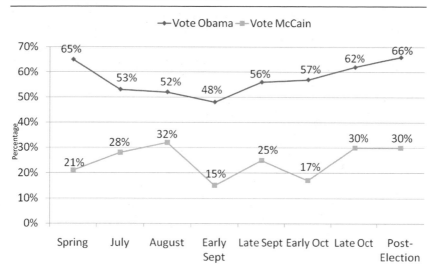

CHART 28. CANDIDATE WILL PROTECT SOCIAL SECURITY

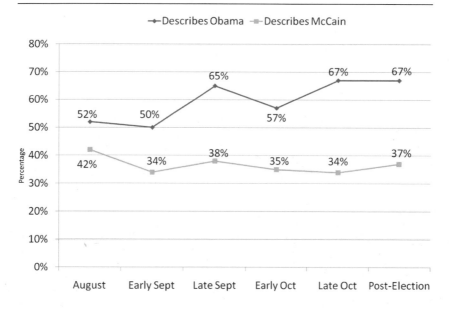

CHART 29. CANDIDATE WILL STAND ON THE SIDE OF THE WORKING PEOPLE

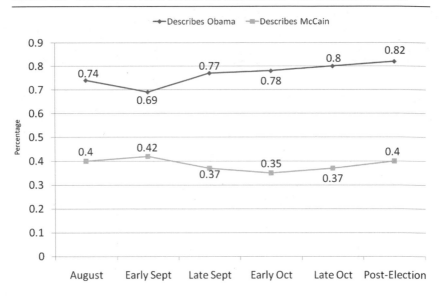

CHART 30. CANDIDATE HAS THE RIGHT IDEAS FOR STRENGTHENING THE ECONOMY

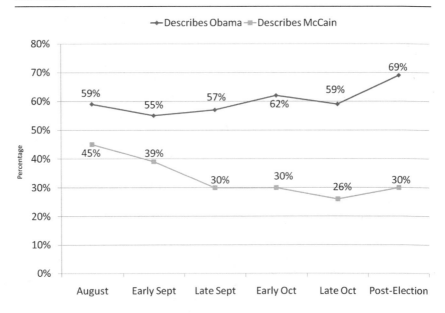

CHART 31. CANDIDATE HAS THE RIGHT IDEAS FOR REFORMING HEALTH CARE

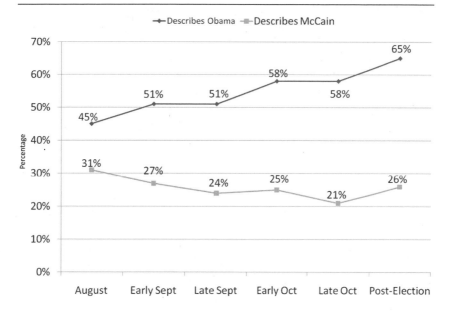

formed by a 26 percent margin for Al Gore, increased to 37 for Kerry and up to 41 for Obama. The question is, "What is the upper limit?"

This is AFSCME-specific polling.

In spring, there was a big margin. [A generic] Democratic candidate versus John McCain. We get to Obama, we're polling in 53–28 and you can see that it narrowed over time. Then as we did our program with repeated mail, particularly in the fall, we drove those numbers up. We ended up with a 66–30 margin.

Positives—same thing. We were able to keep McCain's positives fairly flat-lined and were able to introduce Obama and through the mail, phones, worksite contact, drive up positives for him. . We were [also] able to drive [McCain's negatives] up. They settled back down at the end of the campaign as people made decisions to vote . . . If you think about it—originally it was Barack Obama and his inexperience and John McCain and his economic policies and that's the turf. . . . We focused on the economic policies—McCain, McSame, more of the Bush administration, four more years, we can't afford it.

And these are the last few slides.

You can see a huge difference in the way Obama and McCain were perceived in terms of protecting Social Security; same kind of margin for being on the side of working people.

Right ideas for strengthening the economy. This was the key issue of the campaign. With our members, Obama was winning very heavily there.

And health care. . . .

When you go into a campaign, you have to figure out what kind of resources you're going to put in and how you're going to deploy those resources. . . . We figured we had to drive up McCain's negatives with our members and it was also performance and turnout. Our members turned out to vote because we have a rich history of a political program to make that happen. They perform very heavily for Obama [and] we are thrilled that he is president-elect. We are looking for a worker-family agenda to emanate out of the White House and the Congress in the next four years.

Cecile Richards

Cecile Richards is president of the Planned Parenthood Action Fund, where she oversees engagement in educational and electoral activity, including legislative advocacy, voter education, and grassroots organizing. Richards also oversees the Planned Parenthood Action Fund Political Action Committee, which is committed to supporting pro-choice, pro-family planning candidates for federal office. Previously, Richards served as deputy chief of staff for Democratic Speaker of the House Nancy Pelosi. The daughter of former Texas Governor Ann Richards, she worked with her mother on her very first campaign, the election to the state legislature of Sarah Weddington, the lawyer who successfully argued the landmark 1973 Supreme Court case Roe v. Wade, *which legalized abortion nationwide.*

I'm the president of both the Planned Parenthood Federation of America and also the Planned Parenthood Action Fund and that's really our advocacy and political arm. So the work I'll be talking about today was done through the Planned Parenthood Action Fund.

Planned Parenthood has a special relationship with women in America and worked with that to play an important role in this election. We were focused on educating women voters and that's what I'll be speaking about today.

This is only the second time in our history that the Planned Parenthood Action Fund has endorsed a presidential candidate. For us, the stakes were very high in this election. . . . Planned Parenthood had three goals in the election. One was to elect a president who was supportive of women's health. The second was to expand our majority in the U.S. Senate, to hedge against losing the presidential election because of the [importance of nominations to the] Supreme Court and the stakes for women's health and rights at the Supreme Court and other judicial

CHART 32. PLANNED PARENTHOOD IS THE BEST MESSENGER TO WOMEN

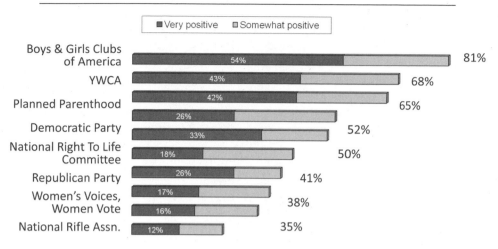

appointments. And the third was to defeat three anti-choice ballot initiatives across the country. I'm just going to talk about the presidential.

Planned Parenthood is one of the most respected, trusted reproductive health care providers in the country. We have 882 health centers across America. We see approximately 3 million women and men through our doors every year. In fact, one in four women in America comes to Planned Parenthood at some point her lifetime. That really was a key part of the relationship we worked with in this campaign; 97 percent of our services are prevention services: cancer screenings, birth control, family planning. This translated into a relationship with women voters that's very, very strong.

We polled early in the election to try to understand the relationship we had with voters and found that, in fact, Planned Parenthood has very high favorabilities among women voters. This was a poll that was done in the early spring with women voters in the battleground states and as you'll see we have a rating that is up there with the YWCA and the Boys & Girls Club of America—much higher than the political parties and usually higher than most of the campaigns and other advocacy organizations.

So we're a trusted messenger on women's health and we felt that this was really important since women were the most sought-after voters in this election. We launched a campaign back in mid-January called the One Million Strong Campaign. The purpose of it was to build on our activist base across the country as well as target a million Planned Parenthood voters whom we could educate and influence in the election.

We polled back in February when it was clear that Senator McCain was going to be the Republican nominee and it was less certain what was going to happen in the Democratic primary.[2] We knew that Senator McCain had a very strong maverick, moderate image not only with the public but frankly with our own Planned Parenthood supporters. Yet we knew he had voted consistently in his 26 years in Congress against women's health care. [He had cast] 125 votes against women's health, [was] adamantly opposed to choice, and in fact had a 0 percent voting record with Planned Parenthood. What we found when we polled women voters was that women had no idea about John McCain's record on women's health. We found that 46 percent of John McCain's own women-supporters were pro-choice, and that three-quarters of women could not even tell you what John McCain's position was on women's health.

So there was a huge education gap here. The other thing we found is that when women got just a little bit of information, they learned that he was opposed to *Roe* [for example] and had voted against women's health care, his support dropped very quickly. In fact, we found when given very little information, 40 percent of his own supporters were less likely to vote for him. So our goal was very simple: to educate women in the battleground states that John McCain was not pro-choice, that he had this long voting record and that he was not supported by Planned Parenthood. Post-election we have learned about polling that was done during the campaign that confirmed what we believed to be true. Once women found out that John McCain was very extreme on women's health issues, it opened up the door for them to get a lot of other information about him that damaged his moderate credentials in the election.

We had several different methods of trying to educate folks about John McCain. We had ten very simple things that we thought every woman needed to know about John McCain, in both English and Spanish.

We had a network of 4 million supporters, we had house parties, we had a whole lot of ways in which that information was given out. We partnered with MoveOn and other progressive organizations to provide viral content that would educate women about his positions.

And then we used very, very limited but targeted paid advertising. We ran ads on "Project Runway," on "Army Wives," on "Oprah," [shows] we felt the voters that we were really targeting were most likely to watch. In the first TV ad we did we took advantage of a media moment. It was an opportunity to show that John McCain was just really out of touch on women's health care issues.

TV Advertisement—"Pause"

ANNOUNCER: Ever use birth control? Then you'll want to hear this:

QUESTIONER: It's unfair—health insurance companies cover Viagra but not birth control. Do you have an opinion on that?

JOHN MCCAIN: I don't know enough about it to give you an informed answer.

ANNOUNCER: Planned Parenthood Action Fund is responsible for the content of this advertising because women deserve quality, affordable health care.

GRAPHIC: Planned Parenthood Action Fund is responsible for the content of this advertising. Paid for by Planned Parenthood Action Fund, www.plannedparenthoodvotes.org. Not authorized by any other candidate or candidate's committee.

We ran this in the summer and it got incredible free media pickup, by the right, by the left, by everybody. Bill O'Reilly did a segment on it and showed our entire ad all over again. There was later a story in the *New York Times* that said that it was this ad and this moment with the press [that ensured that] the sort of open-ended conversation with the press that the straight-talk express actually ended.[3] [After this] they [the McCain campaign] really shut off this sort of open conversation with Senator McCain on issues.

So I think we did strike a nerve. We then did another ad [in response to the controversy over] an ad that was run by the McCain campaign that [said that] Senator Obama essentially wanted to teach sex information to kindergarteners. We felt this couldn't go unanswered and that we were the best organization to speak to it.

TV Advertisement—"Sexual Abuse"

MAN: Every eight minutes a child is sexually abused. That's why Barack Obama supported legislation to teach children how to protect themselves. Now John McCain is twisting the facts and attacking Senator Obama. Doesn't McCain want our children to protect themselves from sex offenders? Or, after 26 years in Washington, is he just another politician who will say anything to get elected?

ANNOUNCER: Planned Parenthood Action Fund is responsible for the content of this advertising.

GRAPHIC: Planned Parenthood Action Fund is responsible for the content of this advertising. Paid for by Planned Parenthood Action Fund, www.plannedparenthoodvotes.org. Not authorized by any other candidate or candidate's committee.

This was a pretty tough ad for us. There was a point at which John McCain's moderate/maverick credentials really got damaged because it seemed he would anything to get elected. I think the nomination of Sarah Palin really confirmed that and reinforced it. In total we ran four ads [and] did an enormous amount of mail, basically just confirming the same health care theme to women. We targeted 600,000 women in the battleground states—to make sure that they understood how out of touch John McCain was and in fact what the difference between him and Senator Obama was.

At the end we are really proud that women voted for Barack Obama by 13 points. I like to think that we had something to do with it. We had seven pro-choice Senate pickups in the United States Senate and we defeated the three ballot initiatives that were on the ballot this year.

Rodger Schlickeisen

Rodger Schlickeisen has held the position of president of Defenders of Wildlife Action Fund since its founding in February 2001. He also has been president of Defenders of Wildlife since September 1991. Prior to joining the organization, Schlickeisen's experience included serving as CEO of Craver, Mathews, Smith & Company, a leading consultancy for progressive advocacy organizations. He served in the Carter White House as associate director of the U.S. Office of Management & Budget, and he was chief of staff to Senator Max Baucus. Schlickeisen is on the board of the national League of Conservation Voters and the LCV Education Fund. He is also a member of LCV's political committee.

I'm president of Defenders of Wildlife and Defenders Action Fund. The Defenders of Wildlife is a large charitable C3 and Defenders Action Fund is a political nonprofit. We're fairly new to the political electoral process.

While he's not great on the environment, McCain didn't have the terrible record that we like to run against. We're much better on the attack than we are on the positive side of things. So he wasn't quite as bad as, say, George Bush was on the environment so it wasn't that appealing a place to go into.

But then he picked Sarah Palin to be the vice president. Sarah Palin is somebody we knew pretty well because there are a lot of conservation issues in Alaska and we knew exactly what she was all about. We were dumbfounded by the choice, as was everybody else. A lot of folks didn't have a lot of research on her, because she's in Alaska. So we watched and tried to figure out what we could do, essentially with no money. We decided to pick on the aerial killing of wolves and bears, but wolves especially, as that was an issue we knew well. We didn't have time to do a lot of polling. But we knew because of our organization's work on the issue that this was an issue that had widespread interest among people. It really touched people where they live.

We were particularly concerned about the women's vote. When we saw the Republican convention in September, they got this huge Palin boost. It actually put them ahead and the Obama-Biden campaign was pretty well frozen. It was unseemly for the Obama-Biden campaign to attack Sarah Palin. The progressive community [was] still kind of learning about her to figure out what could be done to redefine her. They [the GOP] had done a very good job of spinning her and defining her for the public and Republicans thought this was just a wonderful woman.

So we decided we would go first. We had about $35,000. It cost about five or six thousand to make a 60-second ad. We purchased some small buys in Ohio and put it out on the internet.

TV Advertisement—"Brutal"

ANNOUNCER: The more voters learn about Sarah Palin, the less there is to like. As Alaska governor, Sarah Palin actively promotes the brutal and unethical aerial killing of wolves and other wildlife. Using a low-flying plane, they kill in winter when there is no way to escape. Riddled with gunshots, biting at their backs in agony they die a brutal death. And Palin even encouraged the cruelty by proposing a $150 bounty for the severed foreleg of each killed wolf and then introduced a bill to make the killing easier. Do we really want a vice president who champions such savagery?

ANNOUNCER: Defenders of Wildlife Action Fund is responsible for the content of this advertising.

GRAPHIC: Paid for by the Defenders of Wildlife Action Fund. Not authorized by any other candidate or candidate's committee.

We were very gratified by the response to this. The aerial killing
started entering into news stories. For us it had a remarkable response.
We raised over a million dollars in small donations, which we used to
run the ad in six battleground states: We ran it in Ohio, Florida, Wisconsin, Pennsylvania, Colorado, and Michigan and we won all six. We won
all six and all of the evidence that we got back from this was that people
were really touched by this. HCD Research and Muhlenberg College
and Institute of Public Opinion . . . put out an evaluation that said this
was the most effective ad of the election cycle and the only one that
moved voters. We didn't have to have polling in this case because we
knew it would move voters.

That's basically the story. We felt very good about the way it entered
into popular culture. . . . There's an amazingly good and funny rap cartoon made out of it. And, as you probably recall, Tina Fey picked it up
twice in her skits on *Saturday Night Live*. Bill Maher picked it up. The *New
Yorker* had cartoons on it. When the two Canadians called Sarah Palin,
pretended they were the president of France, they said they wanted to
come to Alaska and go shoot wolves out of airplanes with her. So we felt
we're very successful in getting our issue out there and changing people's perception of who this woman was.

[The next ad] is not one that we ran a lot. I was concerned that people
might think that while this [the wolf ad] ad was on target that this really
didn't define her. So I insisted that we make a second ad. One of the
anonymous donors who had contributed to us turned out to be Ashley
Judd. Ashley asked, "Can I do anything else?" I said, "We'd like to make
a polar bear ad; do you want to do the voiceover?" She said, "I'm in
Vancouver making a movie, I've got my sound crew. Send me the
script." So we sent her the script. This was the last ad we did to show
people this [aerial hunting] wasn't a rare, unique experience.

TV Advertisement—"Polar"

ANNOUNCER: The more voters learn about Sarah Palin, the
less there is to like. Scientists say global warming has made
the polar bear highly endangered. But Sarah Palin is fighting
efforts to protect the polar bear, allowing them to be killed
for body parts, for trophies. Do we really want another vice
president with these values?

ANNOUNCER: Defenders of Wildlife Action Fund is responsible for the content of this advertising.

GRAPHIC: Paid for by the Defenders of Wildlife Action Fund.

Not authorized by any other candidate or candidate's committee.

Now, I admit putting "another" [in the ad] was a little snarky but nonetheless we decided [to add it].

BROOKS JACKSON:

Rodger mentioned that they actually made money on one of their ads. I wonder if you had any similar experience of your members increasing donations.

CECILE RICHARDS:

We actually had another sort of political experience with Governor Palin. Someone started a viral e-mail. It wasn't started by Planned Parenthood. It said, "If you are upset about how anti-women's rights and choice she is, don't just get mad, give a contribution in her name to Planned Parenthood."
    We raised more than $1 million in one week and sent 38,000 acknowledgment cards to the McCain-Palin campaign because of the contributions that had been made in her name.

BROOKS JACKSON:

Ricky, you talked about the general election. Of course, in the primary, your union supported Hillary Clinton. There was a time when Hillary Clinton was running out of money that an independent group sprung up, funded largely by AFSCME, if I'm getting it right. Can you tell us a little bit about that independent spending effort to support Hillary Clinton?

RICKY FELLER:

We endorsed her. Once we make an endorsement, we wholeheartedly support the candidates that we endorse. And we were active in numerous states early on going back to Iowa, and contributed to this organization that was running some issue ads.

BROOKS JACKSON:

How effective were they? Do you have any sort of after-action polling on that?

RICKY FELLER:

She didn't get the nomination.

BROOKS JACKSON:

Ultimately, obviously, that's true. (LAUGHTER). Would it have been worse without that? It seemed to narrow the gap in terms of total spending and messaging at a critical time for her. It obviously wasn't enough, but—

RICKY FELLER:

Right. It's hard to say just how effective it was.

BROOKS JACKSON:

Larry, overall, I think you said it was $82 million. Did I hear correctly the figure?

LAWRENCE SCANLON:

$84.2 [million].

BROOKS JACKSON:

$84.2 million. Of that, how much went for independent ads aimed at a general electorate, how much internally?

LAWRENCE SCANLON:

Well, we really did no ads internally [addressing] your membership. I believe it was about $19 million, and that was a combination of hard money and soft money that Ricky spent.

BROOKS JACKSON:

Four years ago, we saw massive advertising efforts. MoveOn was huge. They were nowhere this year really in terms of TV advertising. Media Fund was, I think, funded largely, if not entirely, by labor unions and wealthy donors. Nothing like that this time around—Swift Boat Veterans, Club for Growth on the other side. What do you think accounts for the decline in independent efforts this time around on both sides? Any thoughts on that?

LAWRENCE SCANLON:

One thing is the changes in the law and the FEC regulations regarding electioneering and communications put a little chill, a little fear, into some folks.

CECILE RICHARDS:

I think it was very clear from the outset, once Senator Obama had the nomination, that they were not looking for that kind of campaign. A lot of organizations that might have done more in advertising [instead] spent more time actually working with their membership and running more grassroots campaigns than I think we saw in the last election.

RODGER SCHLICKEISEN

When Mr. Obama decided that he was not going to encourage 527 money, that pretty well dried up the 527 contributions. So there wasn't much you could do without any money.

BROOKS JACKSON:

And by those, you mean big-dollar donations, not just the $25, $50 donations?

RODGER SCHLICKEISEN

Yes, yes, especially the big-dollar donations.

BROOKS JACKSON:

Yes, they discouraged it and that really had an effect on large funds.

CECILE RICHARDS:

Absolutely.

KAREN JAFFE, MACNEIL/LEHRER PRODUCTIONS:

I'm not an expert on McCain-Feingold, so I would like one of you to explain the purpose of the firewall, and also, how do your members understand that? Your members see AFSCME on something that they receive from the union, your members see AFSCME on a television spot, so if you could—it's sort of a two-part question.

RICKY FELLER:

Well, the firewall is put up and taken very seriously. I have a lawyer attached to my hip throughout this whole campaign. What it says is basically that you are required to establish a firewall so that you don't have any contact with candidates, campaign committees, party committees. Anybody that is having conversations with these folks, I was not allowed to talk to.

So for instance, Larry was talking directly with the campaigns. I couldn't talk to him. We set up a thick firewall so that if I was ever brought before the FEC [Federal Election Commission] or whoever [and asked] "Did you ever have a conversation with . . . ?" the answer is no. So it doesn't even get to the next step of, [arguing] "well, but we were talking about this and not this." I'm not sure that gets to the whole question.

KAREN JAFFE:

And the purpose of keeping the two of you apart in terms of the legislation?

LAWRENCE SCANLON:

If you breach the firewall, all the communications that we would have done with soft money to our membership would be deemed basically a contribution to the campaign. Then we would be fined heavily, and would have to use hard money. Obviously, we don't have that much hard money.

KAREN JAFFE:

So the PAC [Political Action Committee] money, obviously, is separate. Your members allocate that money separately from the soft money they're giving the union?

LAWRENCE SCANLON:

Correct. The PAC money is the voluntary money that our members give. We'll probably come close to $15 million over the two-year cycle. That money is used not only for the independent expenditure ads that are express advocacy, advocating the election or defeat of a candidate, but we also use them for contributions to congressional candidates, we use them for contributions to state parties, for the hard money. There're a lot of uses for it, so we husband it very carefully and we're very careful not to have any legal entanglements.

KAREN JAFFE:

You do education to your members so that they understand the differences?

LAWRENCE SCANLON:

Yes. And we've been building our program, particularly over the last 20 years in terms of the PAC, and our members understand it. They work in the public sector for the most part. They have the opportunity to elect their bosses. So when you make the pitch [saying] "It's not only being a volunteer, knocking on doors and making phone calls, but we need a little cash," they come up with it.

RODGER SCHLICKEISEN

Every time you go out there, you seem to be breaking new ground, and you've got attorneys that you're consulting who are trying to figure out whether this is permitted or not permitted. So it's always an exercise in risk assessment, if you will. You don't want to endanger your organization; you don't want to endanger yourself; you don't want to endanger the campaign by doing anything that's wrong. But the law isn't clear about what's right and what's wrong, and so that makes it very, very difficult and also runs up your legal bills.

CECILE RICHARDS:

Absolutely.

LAWRENCE SCANLON:

That's what I was alluding to early on in terms of the changes with the FEC and some of the court decisions. You can use soft money for independent expenditures, but they are issue ads, so you can't expressly advocate the election or defeat of the candidate [in them]. So you have to make a value judgment in terms of risk-reward. If I spend soft money, is it on an issue that is salient to the public? And also, in terms of the longer term investment, if we do an issue ad around Social Security or health care, there's a presumption, at least on our part, that we're going to be moving that agenda forward with whoever gets elected.

BOB CONSTANTINI, CNN RADIO:

One major question is that when Barack Obama raises $700 million, aren't you naturally less inclined to try to help him out and maybe put your dollars elsewhere?

RODGER SCHLICKEISEN:

Yes, I guess to some degree, if they know that money isn't a problem. But I think our groups bring an independent third-party voice. Voters are expecting the campaign to say good things about itself and bad things about the opposition. They're expecting the party to do the same thing. But independent voices are something different and we were very pleased when we got into congressional campaigns in 2006. As with Planned Parenthood, we discovered Defenders of Wildlife favorability was very high. We haven't found a place yet where we didn't rank very, very high. That translates into help for the campaign because you're a credible voice speaking. In some cases, depending upon the issue, [you may be] more credible than the campaign itself.

LAWRENCE SCANLON:

And if I may, this was not a slam-dunk election. Remember, coming out of the RNC convention in early September, McCain was ahead by three points. So you take nothing for granted in political campaigns. You apply whatever resources you need.

CECILE RICHARDS:

To echo what Rodger said, I think the third-party validation is critical and particularly when you have a candidate who is really unknown. Barack Obama was very much unknown. Also with a candidate like Senator McCain we did a lot of our education not around Obama, but, frankly, about Senator McCain. Folks had a certain image of [him] but they basically lacked a lot of really important information, and I think [providing it] was critical in this election. There's a lot of that education that's easier for an outside group to do than for their opponent.

RICKY FELLER:

We were desperate to get a president. We weren't going to leave anything on the table. . . .

RODGER SCHLICKEISEN:

The Obama-Biden campaign couldn't go after Sarah Palin. They knew they couldn't go after her. It would have been very unseemly. It was difficult dealing with a female vice presidential candidate. It was something that the third-party groups could do much more easily.

STEVE WEISSMAN, CAMPAIGN FINANCE INSTITUTE:

Most of them work with America Votes which is supposed to help coordinate interest group activity on the progressive side of these elections. Could you describe what impact the existence of America Votes[4] and their efforts had on your own independent efforts?

And I was wondering if Cecile Richards could tell us how much was spent on the federal aspects of the campaign that she described and whether or not that was mainly small donor financed, or large and small mixed, or how you would describe it.

CECILE RICHARDS:

You want to speak to America Votes?

RICKY FELLER:

I was here in Washington running an independent expenditure campaign just sitting there in what was dubbed "the bubble." So it helped to have contact with America Votes because they had folks within all these states. They served, from my perspective, as a set of eyes and ears and they could help let me know what folks are doing, whether the campaigns that are out there, the party committees, what they were up to, the same thing, and then what some of the other independent expenditure operations are up to. So that's where they helped me out.

CECILE RICHARDS:

I used to run America Votes in the last cycle. I think the purpose there was to say there are a lot of progressive groups that are doing a lot of great work but it doesn't work if everybody's in Ohio and nobody's in

Nevada. The idea was to carve up the work that needed to be done. What you've seen today is a perfect example of an organization figuring out their best purpose in an election, and whether it's working with their membership or the general public. I think that was really the purpose of America Votes.

RODGER SCHLICKEISEN:

A brief comment on America Votes and our experience. They have "tables," the America Votes "table" in each of the states. In New Mexico and Colorado where, as I said, we were very active, we were part of that table. So it was very helpful to coordinate your work at this table in each of the states.

QUESTION:

You mentioned particular shows [in which] you ran ads, "Project Runway." I'm curious what demographic you were looking for? Were those your members? What research do you do to figure out who's [watching?] those shows and what was Planned Parenthood specifically looking for?

CECILE RICHARDS:

We were really focused on independent women and women who were low-information voters and we didn't have a very big media buy. We tried to show our ads in places where we thought they would get some buzz. This was the election of YouTube. So the minute you run an ad, even if you spent $35,000 on it, it's on YouTube. If people hear about it, you get almost as much [impact] virally as you do from that initial run.

We did our limited buys on women's cable that is less expensive, and really targeted the folks that we thought were the getable voters and ones who would appreciate hearing from Planned Parenthood and who didn't have as much information about the election as they probably needed.

BROOKS JACKSON:

Cecile, you mentioned reaching people virally, by e-mail, by YouTube. Do you have any sense, and this is for all of you, whether people reached in that manner are the people who have already convinced? Are you preaching to the choir with this stuff? To what extent are you actually reaching people who are persuadable, undecided, don't know, the way you can with television where you've got to watch this thing if it pops up on the tube?

CECILE RICHARDS:

It's very hard to know. I think that that's the nature of the beast. But it was interesting. One of the groups that we had never really worked with before was MoveOn and as you mentioned, they took a different tact this time. But they actually polled their members to ask what issues you want to know about that you don't know about in this election.

One of the issues that rose to the top was women's health issues and reproductive rights. They called us and said, "Could you do something, a viral piece that we could then use with our members?" For us, it was reaching a whole group that you would think are sort of folks that you had already assumed knew this information but clearly, did not. I think it is difficult to measure, but if you're not in that space, you're not doing politics anymore.

LAWRENCE SCANLON:

It's a process where people are so selective and choose to view the videos, but it's so cheap that it's worth the effort.

RODGER SCHLICKEISEN:

I think it's a mixture. I think people do self-select, but after they find it the viral component is hugely valuable because we had all these stories about somebody who then sent it to their mother, or to their grandmother, or to their aunt saying, "You've got to see this."

RICKY FELLER:

I think as time goes on, we'll be able to measure this. I think right now, it's just hard. You just throw it out there and let it go.

NICHOLAS BALLASY, CNS NEWS:

By Senator Obama opting out of taking public financing, he could raise however much money he wanted basically from whomever he wanted; do you think his campaign will lead to the end of public financing?

LAWRENCE SCANLON:

I don't think so, because he's a very unique candidate and they clearly have the magic elixir, but a lot of other candidates don't have that. . . .

I think there will be some candidates who will want to take advantage of the system.

KATHLEEN HALL JAMIESON, ANNENBERG PUBLIC POLICY CENTER:

A number of your messages included the claim that Senator McCain would tax employer-provided health benefits. They didn't include the statement that said that he would have offset that tax with $5,000 for a family or $2,500 for an individual. Did you discuss that omission before you put the message out? And were you at all concerned that if your target audience realized that that omission was in place, they might have lost some faith in your credibility?

LAWRENCE SCANLON:

When you look at the tax imposed on folks versus the tax credit, it was a net loss for most of the workers, so we felt comfortable in putting out that number.

CECILE RICHARDS:

I think there were so many aspects of Senator McCain's health care plan, at least for the women we were talking to, that were really of concern that it became a big topic, not simply the financial aspect, but the loss of coverage for women, the loss of so many insurance protections that women have fought to get and that they would possibly lose.

I actually feel like that issue became a real drag for Senator McCain. I think his health care plan was particularly [problematic] for women who have more health care needs, and reproductive health care needs that are not always covered. I think his plan ended up being a negative for him in a big way and I think it linked into the economy in a really critical way for our voters.

BROOKS JACKSON:

Just for the record, I think FactCheck.org took issue with what you said about it being a net loss for most workers, but it's an academic question now since McCain won't be pushing it.

Larry, you mentioned that Obama's negatives among your own members was a concern. You showed on the graph how those had risen at about the time of the campaign and then you were able to drive down his negatives. Could you say a little more about that? What kind of negative things were your members thinking or saying about Obama and how did you address them?

LAWRENCE SCANLON:

Well, there're two pieces. There was a favorable impression of McCain. There was less of an impression of Obama because he was unknown. So his [Senator Obama's] negatives when they started, I think were 23 and we were able to bring them down to 17, which was important.

Clearly, race was an issue. We heard that on the doors. There are people out there who vote by race, unfortunately, in this country. We felt we had to address that head on. President McEntee and a number of other labor leaders said to our members, "Look, this is not a black and white issue. It's a green issue. It's about the color of money in your pockets, it's about the economy, it's about jobs, it's about health care." So we had to take that on. We had to deal with the [questions], "Is he a Muslim? Did he swear himself in on the Koran?" all the Internet viral trash that was there. So, yes, that came up and we felt we had to address that head-on and we did.

Notes

1. *Federal Election Commission v. Wisconsin Right to Life, Inc.*, argued April 25–June 25, 2007, http://www.fec.gov/law/litigation/wrtl_sct_decision.pdf.

2. Poll conducted February 12–18, 2008.

3. A. M. Cox, "Turning Points, 2008 Edition," *New York Times*, November 4, 2008, 35.

4. America Votes is a grassroots coalition of more than 40 progressive organizations working to increase voter registration and turnout. http://www.america votes.org/.

Chapter 9
Republican/Conservative Panel

Ed Patru

Ed Patru is vice president for communications of Freedom's Watch, a 501(c)(4) conservative issues advocacy organization founded in mid-2007. Previously, he was communications director of the House Republican Conference, where he helped devise communication strategy for the House Republican minority. He also has worked for the National Republican Congressional Committee as deputy communications director and as press secretary. Patru's political career began in Michigan on the reelection campaign of former Gov. John Engler. He then spent three years doing campaign-related communications for the Michigan Republican Party. In 2000, he worked on the Michigan presidential primary campaign of Sen. John McCain.

Freedom's Watch was formed last year. We're a 501(c)(4) organization. We've been in existence about 20 months. You can basically divide Freedom's Watch's history into two halves. The first half was in 2007. We came out of the gate with a $15 million ad buy on Iraq. Specifically, we came out in support of the surge, trying to make the case to the public that the effort in Iraq was winnable, that the surge was having an impact and, that in effect, it was successful.

We felt that in 2007, you could not have a political or policy discussion divorced from the backdrop of Iraq. In other words, Iraq was, in one way or another, impacting every public policy discussion. So it was very important from our perspective to bring public opinion here in the U.S. more in line with the realities of what was happening on the ground.

In 2008, we shifted focus largely because in an election year there's a lot more focus on a variety of issues. And as Iraq moved off the front pages, and the economy and energy and other issues sort of began to dominate the front pages, our focus began to change as well.

We focused primarily on the issue debates in the House and in the Senate and ended up spending, at the end of the day, a little bit more than $30 million on television, as well as some additional expenditures that we aren't required to report, but 30 million was what was reported on television. . . .

Scott Wheeler

Scott Wheeler is executive director of the National Republican Trust PAC, which came into being September 26, 2008, raising millions to run ads against Barack Obama. Wheeler writes for the conservative site Newsmax and previously worked for Insight *magazine. He is a former television producer and investigative journalist. He has focused on domestic and international security issues and has produced 17 television documentaries and consulted on more than a dozen others. Among Wheeler's work is the video documentary* Trading with the Enemy: How the Clinton Administration Armed Communist China, *released in 2000. He also has focused on the war zones in Yugoslavia and international arms smuggling in Canada, Europe, and the Middle East.*

We got a late start in the election game this year, largely due to just a lack of planning, a lack of an idea that we were going to do this. I think most people coming into this year were expecting Hillary Clinton to run away with the Democratic nomination and that would be that. It would be whatever Republican versus Hillary.

Then the Obama fascination began and that's what really kind of surprised everybody. We didn't know much about him. He was clearly an unknown to everyone except those who had studied his record and studied what little record there was, in addition to the things that he was saying out on the campaign.

And so, about mid-summer, I started toying with the idea of speaking with people I trusted about the potential for getting involved in the election. At that time, we had very little research that indicated bias in the media, but everyone could feel it. As a former journalist myself, I noticed that there were some things about Obama that your average person did not know. I found that to be troubling because as a journalist myself up until that point, I'd always felt it was our job to make sure everyone went to the polls and voted with an informed decision.

So I spoke to Dr. Peter Leitner, who had recently retired from the Department of Defense, and said, "What can we do here?" We came up with the idea of forming a PAC thinking we could raise a little money and run a couple of ads, maybe where it counted, in Ohio or Pennsylvania, or whatever the crucial swing state was at the moment. And so we started putting things together about late August, early September. By just past mid-September, we had the PAC up and running [to the point that] we could start raising money and start planning ads.

We began preparing the first ad when I was shown some polling data about Obama's idea to give driver's licenses to illegal aliens. That Rasmussen poll in 2007 showed 88 percent of Republicans opposed giving driver's licenses to undocumented immigrants; 68 percent of Democrats did; and 75 percent of those without a party affiliation also opposed giving driver's licenses to undocumented aliens.[1] How can you mess with that plan? And so, I'll show you what we ran here and explain the rationale.

TV Advertisement—"Licenses"

ANNOUNCER: Nineteen terrorists infiltrate the U.S.; 14 get drivers' licenses. The 9/11 plot depended on easy-to-get licenses. Obama's plan gives a license to any illegal who wants one, a license they can use to get government benefits, a mortgage, board a plane, even illegally vote.

MAN: Senator Obama, yes or no?

BARACK OBAMA: Yes.

ANNOUNCER: Barack Obama, too radical, too risky.

RNC ANNOUNCER: The National Republican Trust PAC is responsible for the content of this advertisement.

GRAPHIC: The National Republican Trust PAC is responsible for the content of this advertisement. Not authorized by any candidate or candidate's committee.

We took the national security route for two reasons: one, I was a national security reporter and Leitner was a national security specialist. What bothered us about the driver's license for illegal aliens issue itself was probably not what bothered most people in the country. Most people, I think, were bothered by it as a law enforcement issue, an issue that is law and order essentially.

We thought there's even a greater risk allowing people who've come into the country illegally, undocumented. We have no idea who they are, and Obama, as you saw at the end [of the ad], had advocated giving them drivers' licenses. Most people didn't realize that with a driver's license, you can go rent a great, big, gigantic truck, such as what was used in the 1993 World Trade Center bombing and the 1995 Oklahoma City bombing. Most people were unaware that with a driver's license, you can buy guns in many states.

Those are two issues that should be a national security concern because we need to harden our defenses, not lower them. The harder we make it for someone coming into the country illegally with the intent on doing us harm, the harder we make it for them to find a smooth, glide path to legitimacy, the more likely it is we will find out what their intention is, the more likely it is we can find out that they have an agenda other than just coming here to work. So that was the mindset behind the drivers' licenses for illegal aliens ad.

We were taken to the woodshed on it, by the way, by many, including some in this room, for that ad. [Our critics said] that Obama didn't have a plan. Ironically, I found the evidence for this [that he had a plan] in a *San Francisco Chronicle* column last January which warned Obama that he was taking a big risk by advocating for drivers' licenses for illegal aliens. He had at that point a problem with Hillary Clinton who was immensely popular with Hispanics, and she had, I think, about a 59–27 advantage with Hispanic populations. At that time, California was still in play. So Obama, according to the *San Francisco Chronicle*, was taking a big risk by coming out and advocating that kind of program to allow undocumented aliens to have a driver's license.

Well, it didn't become an issue in the general election. McCain didn't make it an issue. We thought this was an important thing to bring up and inform the American people [about], especially since a large portion of those from other polls had determined that many people would change their votes on that issue, and so, an important bit of information. It was not discussed at all in the press in the general election. Once the Democratic primary was settled, that was it. Americans really had no idea where Obama stood.

Next, the ad that I think most Republicans thought McCain should have been running himself was [an ad focused on] Jeremiah Wright, Barack Obama's controversial pastor from Trinity United Methodist Church. And again, that was a little easier subject for this reason. It didn't take writing or arranging because there was Wright on their own released—DVDs saying some very controversial things.

TV Advertisement—"Preacher of Hate"

ANNOUNCER: For 20 years, Barack Obama followed a preacher of hate and said nothing as Wright raged against our country.

JEREMIAH WRIGHT: Not God bless America, God damn America, U.S. of KKKA.

ANNOUNCER: He built his power base in Wright's church. Wright was his mentor, adviser and close friend. For 20 years, Obama never complained until he ran for president. Barack Obama, too radical, too risky.

RNC ANNOUNCER: The National Republican Trust PAC is responsible for the content of this advertisement.

GRAPHIC: The National Republican Trust PAC is responsible for the content of this advertisement. Not authorized by any candidate or candidate's committee.

Many had warned me that running such an ad was going to provoke people to call me racist, which anyone who knows me could not fathom. But there were people who did in the press and it was extremely offensive to me that you're not allowed—I think by the exact opposite, by not dealing with this issue, you have put yourself in a position of being a racist by saying you're not. If that had been an outrageous preacher of any Anglo candidate, it would have been a significant issue and we would have parsed everything he's ever said and you would have that candidate's record of attending church on display for everyone to see.

Saying that it's racist to point this out because it's an African American running for president takes a great deal of chutzpah. We all know that it would not have been this way had it been an Anglo candidate, his church and his minister, particularly in light of what we know Jeremiah Wright said would have been outrageously scrutinized, painfully so.

BROOKS JACKSON:

Ed, you told me, I believe, that your organization is folding its tent here pretty soon. Is that correct?

ED PATRU:

That's correct.

BROOKS JACKSON:

And you're organized as a 501(c)(4), and I think it's correct to say that you can take donations of any size, and that you are primarily a large-dollar-funded organization. Am I right about that?

ED PATRU:

Well, we have a lot of small-dollar donors, but certainly, the big-dollar donors get us closer to where we need to be in terms of putting ads on TV.

BROOKS JACKSON:

So why are you closing up?

ED PATRU:

A number of reasons, but I think far and away the number one reason is the downturn of the economy. I think a lot of our support came from individuals for whom politics is not a livelihood or business. It's an interest or a hobby. Often times, its 10, 12, 15 down on their list, and in tough times a lot of our donors have to make tough decisions. And I think it became increasingly difficult with the downturn of the economy to raise the funds that we needed to remain viable and effective.

BROOKS JACKSON:

And Scott, you're organizing a political action committee. Tell me about your donor base. And did it surprise you that you were able to raise the amount of money you did in so short a time?

SCOTT WHEELER:

Interestingly enough, when we speculated [about] the idea of the Jeremiah Wright ad, we raised $3 to $4 million immediately. We had very few $5,000 donors. Most of our donors were $50, $100, $200 donors and many of them donated two or three times, four times during that three-week period.

BROOKS JACKSON:

And by Election Day, how much did you raise?

SCOTT WHEELER:

We were closing in on 10 million, I believe, coming into the election.

BROOKS JACKSON:

Having registered on September 26.

SCOTT WHEELER:

I was quite surprised.

BROOKS JACKSON:

I sign up for a lot of mailing lists [including] Newsmax, the conservative news site. I was getting a lot of e-mails through them and you were advertising through them. Was that your primary venue for raising money?

SCOTT WHEELER:

In the beginning, yes. We bought their list and mailed it. I was surprised by the results we got from that. Then, once word started getting out, our own Web site surpassed everything else. People were going directly to GOPTrust.com and donating online. Then following the election, we had the runoff in Georgia, which we got involved in, and we raised about another million, 1.2 million for that, and spent close to $1 million in TV ads in Georgia.

BROOKS JACKSON:

Well, I don't know that you've had enough time to look back and reflect on this very much, but what do you think caused this surprising outpouring of cash?

SCOTT WHEELER:

Well, I think there were few other groups doing what we were doing. When I went to Dr. Leitner with this idea, media people I was talking to were saying, "You guys are going to be run out of town on a rail." I went to him and said, "Are you sure you're up to this? You've got a great reputation. I, on the other hand, was a journalist, so nothing is going to hurt me, but you've enjoyed an esteemed career and have many accolades." And he said, "One of the reasons we've been friends for many years is we both have a lot of guts when it comes to this, and what's right is right and this is the right thing to do, informing Americans."

I have to say the attacks weren't as vicious as I expected, but I pointed out to many reporters who called me that our political ads were far fairer to Obama than their editorial coverage of McCain and Palin were. That's a striking dichotomy, a political ad being as fair, or fairer, than journalistic coverage. I can tell by your forum's reaction, Brooks, you don't agree.

BROOKS JACKSON:

Well, we're not here to—

SCOTT WHEELER:

That's another discussion, right?

BROOKS JACKSON:

That's another discussion. We're not here to re-litigate these things. I will say for the record that FactCheck.org found your Mohamed Atta ad to be false on a couple of counts. Obama did not have a plan to issue drivers' licenses. He had spoken favorably of it in the past and you didn't need a driver's license to get on an airplane. Those guys had passports, visas.

SCOTT WHEELER:

That's true, but your argument is with the *San Francisco Chronicle* which called it a plan.

BROOKS JACKSON:

Well, they may not have been correct. But again, we're not here to re-litigate. We did call that a false ad and we'll leave it at that.

I've heard from other groups on the right that were involved in independent political spending that John McCain's stated displeasure with having independent spending groups supporting him really did have an effect on their money. Was that the case with you? You were involved only in state races. Was McCain's stated disinclination to see that sort of thing happen a factor?

ED PATRU:

I don't think so for two reasons: one, for the reason you just alluded to and that is that we weren't involved in the presidential to the extent—

BROOKS JACKSON:

But well, I'm asking, is that the reason you weren't involved?

ED PATRU:

No, it's not. And I'm happy to elaborate on that more if you'd like, but that's the first reason of why I don't think it had an impact is because we didn't involve ourselves in the presidential contest. But the more important reason is that our donors almost categorically gave to our organization because they cared deeply about the issues, whether it was the issue of taxes, energy, card check legislation, or national security, or any other issue that we ran ads on. They fundamentally believed in the positions we had staked out on those issues and that's why they gave.

BROOKS JACKSON:

Okay.

ED PATRU:

So that's a roundabout way of saying that their motivation for giving was larger than any one candidate. It was about a set of principles.

BROOKS JACKSON:

But again, it's primarily the decline of the stock market that you're saying is affecting your donors. They just didn't have the money.

ED PATRU:

I think so. We haven't commissioned a study on it, but my feeling, and there are plenty of other people in our organization who agree with me on this, is that the downturn in the economy had a significant impact on their willingness, even their ability to give.

BROOKS JACKSON:

Yes. Scott, your small-dollar success contrasted with problems with big dollar donors. What does that tell us about the future of independent spending, or does it tell us anything?

SCOTT WHEELER:

Right now, we're preparing to get involved in the Illinois election, the Senate situation with the vacated Obama seat to make sure that the citizens of Illinois get a shot to elect a senator who's not picked for political reasons or, as we've recently found, for other reasons. And so we're going to get involved in the Illinois situation.

So I think, again, the American people have a sincere interest in seeing how their government is run now and if we can play a part in that, it is, I think, very exciting. Maybe independent expenditures are the future of politics because as the media becomes more dispersed, more ghostlike, through the Internet, people are going to be looking for information about elections in ways that previously have been done in a different way, generally sponsored by parties. In '04, we saw the rise of the Swift Boat Veterans for Truth which had a tremendous impact and raised more money than we did over a long period.

BROOKS JACKSON:

They started earlier.

SCOTT WHEELER:

They started earlier. I think we might have beat them if we had gotten two or three months longer, but we will continue to raise these issues and try to inform people of what's going on in these races.

BROOKS JACKSON:

And I wanted to ask you too about the mix of your ads. The driver's license ad, how many times did that appear on the air, as opposed to the Reverend Wright ad?

SCOTT WHEELER:

The popularity of the Wright ad, and the polling suggesting many people did not connect Wright with Obama, is surprising. People in the media probably considered the Wright-Obama connection to be way overdone. Most people did not connect the two. Most people who voted had no idea about Wright and Obama, telling us that if we had been able to get it out a little more and sooner, it could have had even—

BROOKS JACKSON:

But you ran that ad primarily? Was it 10-to-one or two-to-one, what? I know that's the one I saw most often.

SCOTT WHEELER:

Yes, that's the one. I cannot tell you the precise ratio [4:1], but we phased the illegal alien ads down to a smaller percentage because there was a much stronger reaction to the Wright ads.

BROOKS JACKSON:

Yes. Did you have any chance to assess the impact, any sort of discrete polling that might tell us what effect those ads had?

SCOTT WHEELER:

We had none of our own. We did have some that suggested a bump. People who had seen the Wright ad who were undecided, I think seven in 10 broke for McCain, but that was a small sample and we can't really call it scientific, but it gives us some indication.

KATHLEEN HALL JAMIESON, ANNENBERG PUBLIC POLICY CENTER:

Could you tell us where those two ads aired, Scott? And if you were to hypothesize an impact in terms of states, where would you have had the greatest impact?

SCOTT WHEELER:

We did not do a focus group. We didn't do polling or collect it along the way. We were dealing with a short timeframe. Everywhere the illegal alien ad ran the Wright ad also ran.

We had the illegal alien ad probably a couple of weeks before we had the Wright ad, and so our early states [were] Ohio, Pennsylvania, and I believe Nevada and Florida. Then once we had the Wright ad in the can, we realized that we were going to have the money to go national with it. So we started looking at national buys, cable buys, that sort of thing.

MARY GILBERT, *National Journal*:

Mr. Wheeler, you said that Republicans really wanted McCain to bring out the Wright issue himself. But when he started going after Obama for his connections with Bill Ayers, his negatives actually shot way up. So do you think looking back that he really should have gone after Jeremiah Wright or was that something that was better left to third parties to address?

SCOTT WHEELER:

I'm not sure if it's better as a third-party angle. If we had had time to do some really deep research, something I thought would have been sig-nificant would have been a comparison between Obama in Berlin saying, "I'm a citizen of the world" versus McCain in his military uniform with the question, "Don't we want someone to represent America?" We don't need any more citizens of the world. We need somebody to fix our economy [and to] make sure we're protected, who's strong on national security. That's my personal belief.

And so [with] the Wright ad, we felt that people had to know, if people could see what was going on in Barack Obama's church on a regular basis that he attended for 20 years, and in some interviews, in print interviews [he had] said, "Yes, I rarely missed a Sunday," or "I was there almost all the time," undercutting his argument that it was an occasional social event for him. But we felt that the American people would be able to see that. It was clear cut. It was Wright himself and people should have had that information, and polling, of course, showed that most did not.

BROOKS JACKSON:

That brings up something that I wanted to ask Ed about, because you mentioned that the pro-Chambliss ad was a collector's item among independent spenders because it was positive, and I think that's right. In my observation anyway ads run by independent groups are overwhelmingly attack ads. Why is that?

ED PATRU:

Well, for a number of reasons but I think the principal one is that ultimately, the public finds negative ads more believable, more credible, than they do positive ads. For example, if I'm running for Congress and I promise to create 20,000 new jobs in the district, you may or may not believe me; but if my opponent runs an ad saying that I failed to pay my taxes 20 times, and have a number of liens on my business, et cetera, you are much more likely to believe that. So that's one.

And second, ballot results are a factor largely of image, of positive to negative ratio, be it an issue or a candidate or whatever you're trying to impact. When you can affect change on the positive side and affect change on the negative side, you're going to be more successful than when you just focus on either the positive or the negative exclusively.

QUESTION:

Ed mentioned something about the voting ahead of time in Oregon. There seems to be a major trend toward people voting weeks ahead of

Election Day. How is that going to affect your media placement? If you build up to Election Day, you've missed a bunch of voters.

ED PATRU:

Well, I think the biggest impact that will have is that the days of sort of the 11th hour surprise attack ads are going fast, if not gone. It just means the candidates and third parties are going to have to start earlier than ever. If you thought this last campaign was long, wait until four years from now.

SCOTT WHEELER:

It is changing the dynamics of it and it will even change ultimately the campaign strategy itself, apart from media. If you imagine a breaking scandal, if you had one of those states of early voting is a swing state and you're a candidate with a scandal you know is going to break, the longer you hold it off, the more votes you can accumulate before the public is aware of the scandal. And so it's going to change it in many ways, some of which are incalculable at this point.

BROOKS JACKSON:

I should mention that Oregon, of course, is an extreme case because they have only mail voting, through the mails, something they instituted a few years ago. But other states are trending in that direction with more absentee voting, mail-in ballots, etcetera. That's M-A-I-L.

STEVE WEISSMAN, CAMPAIGN FINANCE INSTITUTE:

I just wanted to follow up, Ed, with three things you touched on. I'm wondering if you could expand on why Freedom's Watch focused entirely on the congressional races rather than the presidential at all.

And you mentioned also the non-television ad type, I guess maybe non-radio ad, and why you don't have to report it. I'm wondering if you could give us some idea of how important it was or unimportant it was.

And the other thing is the effectiveness. You were talking just now about ads and what kind of ads are effective. In the previous panel of pro-Democratic interest groups, each group claimed that their ad was terrifically effective in delivering a state for Obama. And because you're on the losing side in the presidential and some—many of the congressional races, can you say something about the effectiveness of your ads or what other influences might have accounted for their effectiveness or lack of effectiveness?

ED PATRU:

Sure. Well, first of all, let me say for the record that we're interested in impacting the issues debate, not in getting particular candidates elected. As a (c)(4), that has to be our focus and that was our focus. Let me try to address the three questions in order. First of all, why we focused on the congressional issue debates as opposed to the presidential. When we started, when the organization started in mid-2007, we built up pretty quickly. And by early 2008, certainly a few months into 2008, we had a staff of several dozen, pushing 50 staff members, a pretty significant research operation, communications, field operation, et cetera.

And so, we had the capacity to involve ourselves in congressional issue debates. I think the difference largely between third-party groups that are focused on Congress and third-party groups that are focused on the presidential is the research component. In a presidential, pretty much all your research is coming out in real time. Every day you open the newspaper, one of the two camps is dropping a new piece of opposition research to reporters. It's getting published.

So, the job of a third party at the presidential level is to basically assemble your favorite issues, poll them, figure out which one moves numbers the most and then run that ad. Whereas, with the congressional, particularly when you're in a (c)(4), you have to get all that research yourself, any quotes, any voting record, any other issues, positions, you have to get that yourself. It's not like as a (c)(4), we're allowed by law to pick up the phone and call the DNC or call the RNC or the NRCC and request their research from them and they can share it. That's all illegal.

So because we had the capacity to do all that research ourselves and a number of other things because of the size of our organization we could do ourselves, we thought that that's where we could have the biggest impact—not to mention the fact that over $1 billion was spent on the presidential election, and so $30 million in the larger scheme of things had a much bigger impact at the congressional level than it did in the presidential.

Your second question, I think, was on nonreported expenditures. That includes Web ads, phones, mail. We think that had a big impact. Mail, obviously, you can target a lot more. You can have a lot more of a narrow focus, much more targeted operation in terms of getting a specific message to a specific demographic that you can't necessarily do with TV. It's much cheaper.

Phones, we had a lot of robocall/live call expenditures going on throughout the summer, almost exclusively focused on the issue of energy. When gas prices were over $4 a gallon, we, every week, had a new set of robocalls going up from anywhere to a dozen—going up anywhere between a dozen congressional districts and three dozen congressional districts.

We thought that any energy plan in Congress had to be comprehensive, and because of that, had to include a drilling component, a domestic drilling component and so we pushed very hard to have members who were opposed to that change their position. We weren't the only ones pushing that issue but I think in terms of supporters of drilling, as part of a comprehensive solution, we were effective.

But, Web, for example, there are some states and districts where we had more expenditures on Web ads. For example, we'd go up in the same week with a Web ad and a cable television address and we spent more on the Web ad than we did on cable and nothing gets picked up by the news, by the media. I think too many reporters and too many districts still don't consider Web ads, even if you're putting more dollars behind them, to have the same kind of weight as a cable address, even though more people may be seeing it. And so, certainly, there were districts where we spent pretty significantly with Web advertising, targeted Web advertising.

QUESTION:

So I wonder if you could talk a little bit about whether you tried to assess the effectiveness of this $30 million program and what you found.

ED PATRU:

Sure. We think the ads, almost all of them, but not all of them, had an impact on the issues which is, again, what we were focused on. . . . At the presidential level, earned media drives everything. Everybody's interested in covering the presidential, the issues that the candidates stake out. Everything they say is covered. But at the congressional level, resources determine how effective you are in getting your message out and the reality is that at the congressional level, conservatives were outspent badly.

I think we had an impact, and I think in many of the congressional districts where we ran issue ads, by the time our issue ads stopped running, the positions, at least publicly, that the candidates were staking out on the issue were—you couldn't really tell the difference. Both candidates were for domestic drilling, both candidates were for lower taxes, both candidates were for not doing anything, for the most part, irresponsible in Iraq. And so I think they did have an impact. So I guess it just depends on how you gauge the definition of effectiveness, whether it's the outcome on the ballot or whether we had an impact on the issues, and I think we did have an impact on those issues.

BROOKS JACKSON:

Let me ask just both of you to sort of pitch forward the idea of independent spending. From what I'm hearing, I think you'd both agree there's a future for independent groups, whether it's (c)(4), 527, whatever. Do you see this thing growing, shrinking? It is going to depend on the candidate, or the issues, or what?

ED PATRU:

When it comes to third parties and effectiveness, you get more innovation and you have third parties that are more effective at doing what they need to be doing when they're out of power in general.

I think one of the reasons liberals and Democrats are light years ahead of Republicans in terms of how they run (c)(4)s and 527s and PACs is because for years, they were out of power and you had the brightest minds in the Democrat Party on the liberal side, out of work looking. It's like a kid. If you leave a kid alone and he doesn't have anything to do, he's going to find something to do. And I think a lot of these very intelligent staffers and long-time consultants or political types on the left put their minds together and came up with some very innovative ways. And so cycle after cycle, they kept improving upon success.

In 2006, I can remember a myriad of 527s and (c)(4)s on the left that were very effective: [with] robocalls, ads, radio ads, mail pieces, et cetera. And on the right, you basically had Club for Growth which, more often than not, aimed its guns at conservatives or Republicans. They will argue that it wasn't a true conservative, but nevertheless, a lot of the casualties came on the Republican side.

So I think now that control of the government has shifted largely to the left, you're going to see a lot of people on the right, a lot of Republicans, many of whom are out of work and looking for something to do, start to devote themselves and dedicate themselves to making these third parties more effective. And so I think eventually, you'll hit parity and it's not out of the realm of possibility, in my view, that in a matter of years, Republicans may surpass Democrats in terms of how effective their third parties are.

SCOTT WHEELER:

. . . . And I think that there is a future for independent expenditures, whether it's us or whoever else, because as Ed also pointed out, you've got people doing one particular thing well and they're focusing a lot of brain power on one particular thing. And whether it's a single issue, or whether it's a broader project defeating a candidate or electing a candidate, whatever it is, you're going to have much more focus on that and much more efficiency and effectiveness using dollars better, raising money easier, that sort of thing.

BROOKS JACKSON:

There was a lot of journalistic fact-checking going on. I think you'd agree not just FactCheck.org, but various organizations. Did this factor into the thinking of either one of you? Scott?

SCOTT WHEELER:

I think the more facts we check, the better off we are. . . . One reporter phoned me and said, "What Obama says, does that really constitute a plan?" My response to him was, "If you are now parsing the definition of the word 'plan' in this campaign, what are we saying about the politicians, that we are so cynical that if they say they're for something, we can't assume they really plan to do it? What are we saying in general?"

And clearly, other people in the press referred to Obama's illegal aliens' thing as "a plan", and that was his proposal. This is what he stood for. He said it in the CNN debate with Wolf Blitzer, very emphatically. That was a controversial, divisive issue, but Hillary Clinton was polling way better than [he was] with Latinos, for example. And he had to do something and everybody knew it was risky, but then, everybody dropped it when it came to the general election.

BROOKS JACKSON:

What I'm hearing is no, it didn't. Ed?

ED PATRU:

I can't speak for other groups, but in terms of Freedom's Watch, we intended from the beginning to be a generational sort of a campaign that extended beyond Election Day. We didn't want to be one of these one-cycle shows that dissolved after Election Day, didn't really care about our credibility, et cetera. We wanted to be around for years, if not decades.

And so, every ad that we ran, what we kept at the forefront of our mind was credibility, long-term credibility. For example, Swift Boats for Veterans [for Truth] ran very effective ads, but it was very doubtful they could have had much of a future after the Election Day because of how hard-hitting their ads were and how so many of the public perceived that their ads pushed the envelope too far.

BROOKS JACKSON:

They were very specific to John Kerry anyway.

ED PATRU:

Sure but the more hard hitting, the more effective an ad is. Many times I can tell you [that] we erred on the side of caution for one reason, and one reason only, and that was because the credibility of our organization was paramount for us. It wasn't until this month that we realized that we were probably going to have to close our doors. What guided us all along was credibility.

BROOKS JACKSON:

Scott, about the Jeremiah Wright ad, we've heard from the McCain folks that John McCain absolutely ruled this out, didn't want to do it. . . . Give us some idea of how you came to the notion that you should run this ad that John McCain didn't want to run.

SCOTT WHEELER:

The fact that we knew that he didn't and wouldn't was one clue that it was a very important issue, something that the American people needed to know about, especially with Senator Obama, who had a blank slate. I think many analysts have pointed out that Obama was a blank canvas and people were painting whatever they wanted. I had e-mails from people, and I've heard this backed up in other news accounts, people thought that they weren't going to have to pay for gas if Obama was president.

And I thought, "How on earth are they thinking that?" And Obama being a blank slate, someone had to show what has informed his opinions over the years. Someone had to say this guy has had some very controversial friends, Bill Ayers and Jeremiah Wright, just two of the most prominent. And so we said, "McCain is not going to mention this. There's a place for this ad here and the American people need to know that questions need to be asked." The press wasn't asking them.

BROOKS JACKSON:

I think in the end, you were running that ad on MSNBC even.

SCOTT WHEELER:

Yes.

BROOKS JACKSON:

You had so much money, were there any persuadable voters for you watching MSNBC?

SCOTT WHEELER:

You'd never know. I think you really can't tell. I know that—

BROOKS JACKSON:

You were looking for open slots to run that ad, just to spend the money, right?

SCOTT WHEELER:

Well, we were. As we were coming down, we were leaving no stone unturned and we wanted to try to influence everyone we could.

BROOKS JACKSON:

I guess here's what I'm wondering. McCain clearly made a decision that [focusing on] Jeremiah Wright would not help him, so did you run that ad to help John McCain or to help your own fundraising, just to put it bluntly?

SCOTT WHEELER:

No, it had nothing to do with fundraising. We wanted to inform and explain to them, here's a guy running for the highest office in the land and here's what his minister thinks about this country and this government. I cannot overemphasize the importance of that information to someone voting for Barack Obama who spent 20 years in that church.

Note

1. Rasmussen Reports, November 4, 2007, "77% oppose drivers' licenses for illegal immigrants," http://www.rasmussenreports.com/public_content/poli tics/current_events/immigration/77_oppose_drivers_licenses_for_undocument ed_immigrants.

Index

Italics indicate photographs and charts.